F55

Finishing Touches
JEAN KERR

DOUBLEDAY & COMPANY, INC., GARDEN CITY, NEW YORK
1974

A portion of this work (Copyright © 1973 by Jean Kerr) appeared in BEST PLAYS OF 1972–1973. Edited by Otis L. Guernsey, Jr. Published by Dodd, Mead & Company, Inc.

Lyrics from "That Old Gang of Mine" (pp. 21, 161), Billy Rose, Mort Dixon and Ray Henderson, © Copyright 1923 Bourne Co., New York, N.Y. Copyright renewed. Used by permission.

Library of Congress Cataloging in Publication Data
Kerr, Jean Collins.
Finishing touches.

A play.
I.   Title.
PS3521.E744F5   1974   812'.5'4
ISBN 0-385-02713-3
Library of Congress Catalog Card Number 74-3474

Copyright © 1972 by Collins Productions, Ltd.,
David J. Cogan and Frank Collins, Trustees,
Jean Dolores Kerr and Mrs. Thomas J. Collins
All Rights Reserved
Printed in the United States of America
First Edition

For Josephine—who knows why
With love

CAST OF CHARACTERS

JEFF COOPER, *a university professor*

KATY, *his wife*

KEVIN, *their son, eighteen*

HUGHIE, *their son, eleven*

STEVE, *their son, twenty-two*

FELICIA ANDRAYSON, *Steve's girl, twenty-six*

FRED WHITTEN, *a professor friend and neighbor*

ELSIE KETCHUM, *a student, twenty-two*

SETTING

(*The living room of the* JEFF COOPER
*family in a university town in New
England, with a dining area at down-
stage Right. The house was built by
someone who had money, but* JEFF
COOPER *is a university professor, and
it now looks comfortably shabby. The
front entrance is at stage Left but not
quite within view, being recessed in
a small foyer. Below this entrance
foyer is a hall closet, with a spring
door that closes automatically. The
family telephone is inside the closet.
Above Left, and beneath the stairwell, is a window-seated game alcove
with a chess set in place. Scattered in
the same area are the wires and gim-
micks belonging to* HUGHIE'S *tape*

recorder. *The staircase is against the back wall, beginning just Left of center and rising toward Left. To Center and Right of the back wall is an entrance to the outdoor terrace, with wide glass doors. When the terrace doors are open, we can see part of a long redwood table on the flagstones. Just below the terrace, angled toward Right, is a window looking toward the terrace and garage. Below it is a door Right to the kitchen. And down Left there is a door to* JEFF's *office. Otherwise there is a fieldstone fireplace with a large philodendron set into it, a sofa, casual chairs, a bookcase with a desk shelf. A string of Christmas tree lights is inexplicably draped over the stair-case rail*)

The time is the present

ACT ONE: Breakfast
ACT TWO: Late afternoon
ACT THREE: Evening

(*The lights are lowered during Act Three to denote a lapse of twenty minutes*)

Act One

AT RISE: FOUR MEMBERS *of the family are at*
            breakfast. The parents, KATY *and*
            JEFF COOPER, *are reading sections of*
            the morning newspaper. KEVIN, *a*
            high school senior, is poking away at
            his food. HUGHIE, *eleven, is playing*
            with a cash-register bank.

HUGHIE

Mom, you owe me a nickel. Will you give me a nickel?

KATY

(*Not looking up.* KATY *is a very pretty*
woman and SHE *will look better when*
SHE *gets out of that frowsy bathrobe*)
What do I owe you a nickel for?

HUGHIE

I took all the Coke bottles out of the garage.

KATY

(To JEFF, *who has not been listening*)

Honey, we owe him a nickel. Give him a nickel, will you?

JEFF

What do we owe him a nickel for?

KATY

(SHE's *not going over that ground again*)

Just give him a nickel. Okay?

(HE *reaches into his pocket for one*)

KEVIN

You know, the President's statement is bound to worsen the international situation.

KATY

You're absolutely right. Now eat your eggs.

KEVIN

Don't you care about the international situation?

KATY

I care terribly; now eat your eggs.

KEVIN

If you'd look, Mom, you'd see I'm not eating eggs. I'm eating french toast.

KATY

Are you trying to start an argument?

KEVIN

Oh, Moth-*er!*

KATY

I was only eighteen years old when your brother Stevie was born. Never forget that.

KEVIN

Yeah, but what are you going into that for?

KATY

Because you seem so big, so massive. And you soak up so much oxygen. I feel I must be at least sixty-five.

KEVIN

Well, we can figure this out. You were eighteen when Steve was born and Steve is twenty-two now. That makes—

KATY

(*Interrupting*)
Never add in my presence. I'm high-strung.

HUGHIE

You know, Mom, your neck looks fine from the front. But from the side it looks like sort of twisty.

KATY

I hate breakfast anyway. Why do I eat breakfast? Look, if you will be silent, I will see that you get another nickel. Two nickels.

HUGHIE

I don't need another nickel.
>   (HE *places the nickel* HE *already has*
>   *in the bank and there is a sudden*
>   *small explosion*)

JEFF

My God, what's that?

HUGHIE

It's my bank. It hit twenty dollars. I mean it's supposed
to be twenty dollars. Boy, if it isn't twenty dollars—
>   (*Starts counting coins*)

five, ten, fifteen—Do you suppose I could sue them if it's
not twenty dollars? Twenty, twenty-five, thirty—

JEFF

You're not going to count that whole damn mess?

HUGHIE

Sure. How will I know if I—?

JEFF
>   (*Interrupting, very quietly*)

Look, I will give you twenty dollars and I will take all
those coins.

HUGHIE

But it might be more than twenty dollars.

JEFF

I will give you twenty-one dollars.

HUGHIE

Honestly, Dad, I've got to count them.

JEFF

Okay, you will count them.
> (HE *starts gathering them up with his*
> *two hands and dumping them into a*
> *cereal bowl*)

You will take them up to your bedroom after school and you will count them.

HUGHIE

That bowl's still got cereal in it.

JEFF

Before you count them, you can wash them.

KEVIN

Dad, you drink too much coffee, you really do.

JEFF

I also smoke too much. Now eat your eggs.
> (KEVIN *holds plate out*)

KATY

I always get the rotten half of the paper.

JEFF

Well, every day we take a different half.

KATY

That's why it's strange that I always get the rotten half.
> (*Phone rings and* KATY *jumps up*)

JEFF

Katy, there's no point to jumping at every phone call. I told you. Dean Dennis will not be calling me. They send you a special delivery letter.

> (HUGHIE *has gone to answer the phone
> in the closet*)

KATY

But you will get it today?

JEFF

In theory, yes. The letters arrive the day before Memorial Day.

KEVIN

Nobody in the world but us keeps the telephone in the clothes closet.

JEFF

That's where it was when we bought this house. We just never moved it.

KATY

And it has advantages. We don't have to listen to Hughie's conversation.

JEFF

And you can't talk too long or you'll smother.

HUGHIE

> (*Reappearing from the telephone
> closet*)

That was Sam. He just wanted to know what the arithmetic homework was.

JEFF

Today's homework?

(*Suddenly* HUGHIE *is agitated, rushing about to pick up his school things*)

HUGHIE

Oh, I'm going to be late and Miss Barnes will kill me. And you know why I'm gonna be late? Because I can't ride my bicycle. The tires are flopping again. That's because Kevin takes it and he rides his fat girl friend on the handlebars and do you think in one million years he'd ever get it fixed? Oh, no, not him, he'd—

KEVIN

Why don't you pipe down and button your shirt and zip your pants?

HUGHIE

Tell him he can't use my bike! Tell him he can *not* use my bike for fetching and carrying this—

KATY

(*To* KEVIN)

You cannot ride your fat girl friend on Hughie's bike.

KEVIN

Angie weighs one hundred and five pounds.

HUGHIE

Which half?

JEFF

Miss Barnes will not kill you. I will kill you if you don't get out of here!

HUGHIE

I'm going. Where's my science project?

KATY

If you mean that piece of cardboard that's got little stones glued all over it, it's on the window seat where you left it. Here, don't forget your lunch.
(HUGHIE *grabs the lunch roughly*)
Hey, don't grab it that way! You'll smash the cookies.

HUGHIE

The milk money—?

KATY

Is under the sandwich. And eat the sandwich first. Okay?

HUGHIE

(*Patting his coat pocket*)
My pen feels like it's not here. Kevin, did you—?

KEVIN

I did not *touch* your crutty pen.

HUGHIE

Well, it's very mysterious. Mom, do you know what I need, do you know what I really and truly need? A new poncho. My poncho doesn't keep the rain out. I could just as well wear a couple of pieces of Kleenex.
(*Starts to get it*)
I'll show you.

KATY

No, you will not show me. You haven't got time to show me. We'll talk about it later. Hughie, honey, will you do me a favor? Will you please do your poor old mother a favor? Will you go? Will you please go? Will you go now?

HUGHIE

Okay, but we're getting very tense all of a sudden.

JEFF

It's *not* all of a sudden.

HUGHIE

(*Departing finally, using front door*)
Well, all right, good-bye.
(HE *flicks something near his tape
recorder in passing*)

KEVIN

That kid is retarded. He must be the youngest eleven-year-old boy in America.
(HUGHIE *is gone, but suddenly there
is the loud blare of an old recording,
"That Old Gang of Mine," bleating:
"Good-bye forever, old fellows and
        gals,
    Good-bye forever, old sweethearts
        and pals—"
It continues. The Christmas tree
lights blink on and off*)

JEFF
(Jumping before the second line)
My God, what is that?

KEVIN
Hughie's recorder.

JEFF
Hughie's? Why isn't it up in his bedroom?

KATY
He got those Christmas tree lights out of the attic.

JEFF
Get it off! Turn it off!

KATY
(Who has run to the tape recorder near the game table)
I don't know how to turn it off! Where does it turn off?
(Fiddling, SHE is making it louder)

KEVIN
(Hurrying to her rescue)
It's this button right here.
(HE gets it off. Pause to taste the silence)

JEFF
Will you tell me how he arranged that?

KEVIN
He's got it connected to a timer.

JEFF

A timer? Where does that kid get the money for all this junk?

KATY

He's got a paper route.

JEFF

He should give up the paper route. Or maybe we should make him pay board.

KATY

Honey, calm down!

KEVIN

Mom, I've got a meeting after school so I won't be home for supper. What can you leave in the oven?

KATY

My head.

KEVIN

It's okay—I'm laughing inside. Now where's my soc-sci book. I left it on this shelf. Here it is.

KATY

Your what book?

KEVIN

Soc-sci. Social science. Mom, I've told you that a hundred times. Don't you remember anything?

KATY

I remember a lot of things. Gutenberg invented the print-
ing press. The formula for water is H_2O. Eleanor of
Aquitaine died in twelve hundred and four—
> (KEVIN, *having found his book, is*
> *on his way out*)

JEFF

Kevin, say good-bye to your mother and, if you can manage
it, me. Remember what Auden says. Man is the only animal that learns by being hypocritical. He pretends to be
polite and then, eventually, he *becomes* polite.

KEVIN

Dad, you *always* sound like a professor.

JEFF

I sound like a professor because I am a professor. That's
one of those occupational hazards.

KEVIN

Very well. Good-bye.
> (*With a flourish*)

God ye god den, gentle Mother. Farewell, sweet Father.
> (*Flourish over*)

See you around.
> (KEVIN *goes.*
> *There is a pause before* KATY *speaks*)

KATY

You remember how terrible we felt that we couldn't have
more children?

JEFF

I can remember how terrible I felt that I was too young to shave. Some things you get past. Do we know whether Steve is coming home this weekend?

KATY

Not yet we don't. It's too bad this isn't a hotel. Then he'd have to make a reservation.

JEFF

I've got to get dressed. How I hate these morning classes. Everybody half asleep, including me.

KATY

Have some more coffee. Sit for a minute.

JEFF

You heard Kevin. I'm drinking too much coffee now.

KATY

You know you haven't talked to me in weeks.

JEFF
(*Giving her a peck on the top of the head*)
Okay, you brood about that.

KATY

But it's true! You talk *at* me, through me, past me. But you don't listen. I feel like Muzak—something that's piped in to be part of the background. You look worried—no, not worried, abstracted—as though you had just lost your car keys.

JEFF

You're the one who loses car keys.

KATY

See! You're saying the first thing that came into your head.
You're not even looking at me!

JEFF

All right, I'm looking at you now. Burn that bathrobe. Or
give it to the poor. No, they're poor enough.
(*Heading upstairs*)
I have to get ready. And will you please tell me why Kevin
keeps taking my ties? Kevin doesn't wear ties.
(JEFF *vanishes upstairs.*

KATY *sighs, begins to pick up dishes,
then looks into the mirror on the
wall.* KATY *has a habit of talking to
herself*)

KATY

Well, I may not be gorgeous, but I do have great bones.
And if I'd get a little weight off you could see the great
bones. Some day I shall win a lottery. I know that because it has been revealed to me in a dream. And after I
pay off the mortgage on the house, I'll spend all the rest
of the money at the Golden Door or someplace where
loving hands work on you night and day. And when I get
out after six or seven months, strange men will breathe
heavily when they see me at the check out counter at the
A&P.

JEFF

(*From above*)

Honey, will you stop talking to yourself and find me my raincoat?

KATY

It's not going to rain.

JEFF

On Channel 5 it's raining.
(*Comes down holding two ties in front of him*)
Which tie is better with this suit?

KATY

The brown one, I guess.

JEFF

No, I am too brown already. I look like a big Hershey bar. Now where are my glasses?

KATY

I didn't know your glasses came. When did they come?

JEFF

I picked them up yesterday.

KATY

Well, put them on and let's see them!

JEFF

They're just glasses.

KATY

But it's sort of an event. Your first pair of glasses!

JEFF

Why don't we wait until I get my first hearing aid? Then we can have a cake with candles.

KATY

Put them on.

JEFF

I only have to wear them for reading!

KATY

Put them on.
(HE *puts them on, finally*)
Well, now, I think you look very distinguished.

JEFF

(*Sharply, taking them off*)
Who the hell wants to look distinguished?

KATY

Jeff, honey—what's the matter?

JEFF

Nothing.

KATY

But, my dear, there is something the matter. I woke up at five o'clock and you were sitting in that green chair staring out the window and you looked so sad and I couldn't speak to you because I felt I had stumbled onto something private.

JEFF

It's nothing. I don't sleep well. Lots of people don't sleep well.

KATY

(*Running her finger over his fore-head*)

Okay, but we've got to get rid of this little frown. It's turning into a furrow. And you mustn't have got the brush wet enough because those little hairs are sticking out in the back.

JEFF

(*Pulling away with a real explosion*)

Will you for God's sake stop patting me!

KATY

(*Stung*)

All right. Certainly.

JEFF

(*Quickly putting his arms around her*)

Oh, honey, honey, honey—I'm sorry. The truth is, I *am* jumpy. But I don't have to take it out on you. You hurt?

KATY

Oh, just a little, maybe. But that's a reflex, I'll get over it. What I want to know is why you sort of avoid me lately.

JEFF

Where did you get that crazy idea?

KATY

It's not crazy. You always used to come home a half hour early from school so we could have a little drink together before the kids got here. You haven't done that in months.

JEFF

Of course, the whole business of my promotion has come up. And notice—I still haven't heard.

KATY

For a while I thought that was it. But it isn't it. And I used to like it when you got through your papers at eleven o'clock and you'd come out of your study and say, "Hey, if you'll walk with me to the post office, I'll buy you a corned beef sandwich." How long is it since you've done that?

JEFF

My God, if your idea of a big thrill is to walk to the post office—

KATY

(*Close to tears*)

People settle for things. Don't you understand? They *settle*. I'm beginning to feel like a nonperson. And yesterday —yesterday you called me "Mother."

JEFF

Well, there. Now we've got something really important to be upset about!

(FRED WHITTEN *has just wandered
in through the terrace without their*

noticing. FRED *is a law professor who rents the apartment above their garage.* HE *realizes* HE *has interrupted a quarrel, though it doesn't faze him*)

FRED

Hey, what's with the beautiful people?

JEFF

(*As* HE *and* KATY *break apart, a little embarrassed*)

Oh, Fred, it's not bad enough that you're underfoot all the time. You lurk.

FRED

Properly speaking, one lurks in bushes or behind trees. I don't think you can lurk in here.

JEFF

It's hard, but you manage. The next time I'll rent that garage apartment to an enemy.

FRED

(*To* KATY, *who is heading for the stairs*)

Where are you going?

KATY

I'm just going to get dressed.

FRED

I'm sorry about that. I've grown accustomed to that bathrobe. It has that *fin de siècle* air that's become so scarce since the end of World War One.

KATY

(*Cross, but it's* JEFF SHE *is cross at*)
Fred, honey, please. Just for today, knock it off, will you?
(SHE *goes upstairs*)

FRED

What's with our girl?

JEFF

Oh, what's with everybody?

FRED

That's another question. I want to know about Katy.

JEFF

I guess I upset her.
(*Stops gathering papers for school
and turns to him*)
Fred, let me ask you something. How do you feel about
being forty?

FRED

Oh, I get around without a cane and I have my own teeth.

JEFF

That isn't what I meant. Do you ever feel that you'd like
to get out of teaching and do something else before it's
too late?

FRED

You haven't heard yet? Whether or not you're going to
be made a full professor?

JEFF

No.

FRED

Are you worried that you won't? Or is it possible that you're worried that you will.

JEFF

I'm not sure, I don't know. But you didn't answer my question. Do you ever think you'd like to be doing something else?

FRED

Like what else?

JEFF

Oh, manage the Mets. Own a motel. Open a pet shop.

FRED

You forget that I spent eighteen months after I got out of the Army bumming around Mexico. At the time it seemed like a high-spirited lark. Now all I can remember is the dysentery.

JEFF

But you did it.

FRED

Yes, but I wouldn't do it now. Besides, I like teaching. I like the students. I like having them drop in at all hours of the day and night. It's probably why I have trouble keeping a wife.

JEFF

I forgot to ask you. When is Helen coming back?

FRED

Well, she was going to spend a week with her mother and then she wrote that her mother had a cold and she was going to spend an additional week. Today I heard Mother has bronchitis, which means that Helen will have to stay longer. Now, we are all mortal and subject to respiratory ailments, but it sounds suspiciously like an old pattern to me.

JEFF

You're wonderfully calm about it.

FRED

Actually, I don't know why I married Helen. I swore I'd never have another wife. You get so attached to them.

JEFF

Why *did* you marry her?

FRED

Well, she suggested it. And there didn't seem any polite reason to say no. I *had* the room.

JEFF

All these years and I don't really understand you. You're not superficial. Are you just callous?

FRED

No. I am that careful. When I came home from Korea

I found that Sally was in love with, living with, an oculist. You can imagine the jokes. What does he see in her and so forth. Except that I didn't find it very funny. It seemed to me that my heart broke. That's what I was doing in Mexico for eighteen months—trying to reassemble the pieces. And then I was all right but not all right. But I knew that I couldn't go through that again—and I haven't.

JEFF

Sally didn't marry the eye doctor, did she?

FRED

No, but that didn't help. I married Claire and that didn't help, either. And now we've dealt with the purple passages in my life. What the hell is the matter with you?

JEFF

Wouldn't it be nice to know. Do you think I could be losing my mind?

FRED

I doubt it, but why do you ask?

JEFF

Well, I'm developing strange new patterns. For instance, I bring my last drink upstairs to bed with me. Because by the time I've got through checking everything I'm almost sobered up again.

FRED

What do you check?

JEFF

Everything. Katy's cigarettes. She never puts them out. The thermostat. I move Hughie's bike so the milkman won't fall over it and I turn off Kevin's radio. But that isn't the point. I take this drink up. But last night I couldn't find it. It wasn't in the bathroom, it wasn't on top of the dresser. So I retraced my way back through the whole house. I even went out to the garage. But I couldn't find the drink.

FRED

Why didn't you make yourself another one?

JEFF

That's just it. I couldn't. It seemed absolutely vital that I find this particular drink. I was convinced—you understand it's now four o'clock in the morning—I was really convinced that if I didn't find this particular drink, nothing would ever be right again. And I didn't find it. And this happened—oh God, a number of times, a *lot*.

FRED

Okay, the nights are bad. What else?

JEFF

Fred, old buddy, do you know there was a time when if I could get one of those boys from the engineering school to recognize a heroic couplet, I thought I was materially adding to the sum of human knowledge? Now I'm not so sure. And little things exasperate me. Do you see that Clorox bottle in front of the plant?

36

FRED

Yeah.

JEFF

What do you suppose it's there for?

FRED

Katy is trying to bleach the rhododendron.

JEFF

No, she uses it as a pitcher to water the plant. Wouldn't you think she'd put it back? She only waters the plant about once a week. Why does it have to sit there?
> (*Gets up to take it to the kitchen*
> *himself, is deflected by the sight of*
> *the cups on the coffee table*)

And have you ever noticed our cups? They don't match the saucers. They don't match anything! That's because the boys break the cups. I don't know how many sets of dishes we've had since we were married, but the cups always go first. So Katy goes to the five-and-ten and buys cups, which would be all right if she bought saucers to match. But she won't do that because, you see, we *have* saucers! And you can't find a drinking glass in the cupboard because it's so full of Santa Claus mugs!

FRED

I see. Even the dishware bothers you. How is your sex life?

JEFF

What? I mean I heard you. I'm not really prepared to go into that. But I may say that for two people who haven't had a decent night's sleep in six months, we both get sleepy at the damndest times.

FRED

Well, we have an extra set of dishes—all matched—in a crate in the basement. You're welcome to them, though I don't promise they'll help you to sleep.
(*Pointing to the table*)
What's this hammer doing here?

JEFF

Hughie likes walnuts for breakfast.
(KATY *returns from above, dressed in jeans and sport shirt.* SHE *has obviously determined to be bright and cheerful for* FRED's *benefit*)

KATY

Fred, I'm glad you're still here because I forgot to congratulate you.

FRED

On what?

KATY

On your review of the Plautus play.

JEFF

Oh, *The Menaechmi.* Did you review it?

KATY

My dear, he reviewed it in Latin.

FRED

Well, the kids performed it in Latin—without intermission, I may add—on the steps of Caldwell Hall. It gave a new meaning to the word "interminable."

JEFF

It's like I was saying before you came in, things are tough all over.
(*Putting things into his briefcase
again*)

FRED

(*Remembering that little scene*)
Oh yeah, yeah—look, I came over to check something in your *Oxford Companion*. Somebody borrowed mine. And before you say anything, I will not borrow yours. I will leave it right on the desk.

JEFF

(*Calling after him as* HE *goes into
den, shutting the door*)
What I wish you'd borrow is the lawnmower and cut your half of the grass.

KATY

(*Once* FRED *has closed the den door*)
Jeff, I want to apologize.

JEFF

For what?

KATY

For giving you the third degree. About nothing. You should be allowed to have a mood once in a while. I'm a pest and there is nothing the matter with you.

JEFF

Katy, there is something the matter.
(*Slight pause*)
I think I'm falling in love.
(*The phone rings.* JEFF *quickly turns and goes to answer it in closet*)

KATY

(*Alone*)
I must say nothing. Nothing at all, not one thing. Because anything I say is going to be a mistake, a serious mistake. But I'm here. I can't run upstairs and hide in the bedroom. I have to say something. Above it . . . rise above it!

JEFF

(*Returning from telephone closet*)
Want to know what that was?

KATY

Not particularly. Now you were saying what? That you were falling in love? Is that all?

JEFF

Is that *all*?

KATY

My God, from your expression I thought you had stolen

money from the university. Or you just discovered you had hepatitis.

JEFF

Well, I'm glad to be able to put your mind at ease.

KATY

Look, I'll try to take you seriously, but I don't believe that men get to be your age and suddenly change the patterns of a lifetime.

JEFF

Sure they do. Bernard Shaw didn't even start to write plays until he was forty years old.

KATY

That's different from chasing girls.

JEFF

Yeah—harder.

KATY

Well—who is the girl?

JEFF

She's in my poetry seminar.

KATY

And what's so special about her?

JEFF

The terrible thing is, I don't think there's anything special about her. I noticed her in the first place because she was the only one in the class who didn't say anything. I thought it was because she was so shy. It now strikes me that she wasn't shy at all. She just hadn't read the assignment.

(KATY *manages a small smile*)

It's all right, you can smile. I think it's funny.

KATY

I suppose she's terribly pretty.

JEFF

No, not really. Oh, she's pretty in that sort of nothing way that airline stewardesses are pretty. You know how they look. They've got straight noses and good teeth, so you've got to say they're pretty, but they sure as hell don't look like the ads. I mean, she wouldn't bowl you over.

KATY

But she bowled you over. Why?

JEFF

I don't know. I honest to God don't know. She laughs a lot.

KATY

Of course, you're not terribly funny around here. But I suppose once out of the nest—

JEFF

No, you don't understand. She laughs because she's happy. She still thinks everything is possible. And she notices things.

KATY

Like what?

Oh, things that have always been there but you just didn't see them.

KATY

Of course, now that you've got your glasses—

JEFF

(Ignoring that one)

You know that statue of Beethoven in the library? She said it looked like Dean Dennis watching a basketball game. And with that scowl, it really does. And yesterday she showed me how the cracks in the wall behind my desk look like a pair of folded hands.

KATY

With her fine sense of observation, has she noticed that you're married?

JEFF

That's just what you'd say, all right. You don't understand. To her I'm just a dreary professor who teaches "From Beowulf to Spencer." She doesn't know that my heart stops when I see her at the water cooler. I get coughing spells. It's the most ridiculous thing. And all the while I'm droning on about the beauties of Beowulf in its majestic and contrapuntal harmonies—God, what a boring poem that is and when will I have the nerve to say so?—all the while I'm thinking how wonderful it would be to be on a narrow sandy road in Bermuda, riding a bicycle with Elsie.

KATY

Her name isn't really Elsie?

JEFF

That's right, her name is Elsie. Elsie Ketchum. You see how everything conspires to make this whole thing preposterous.

KATY

And you've never ridden a bicycle.

JEFF

That's right.

KATY

You could practice on Hughie's after he gets it fixed.

JEFF

Katy, nobody has fantasies about things they've already done.

KATY

I wouldn't know. I don't have fantasies about anything.

JEFF

I don't believe it.

KATY

I don't.

JEFF

You've never imagined yourself in a strange city hurrying to meet somebody new? Wouldn't you like to have somebody notice the color of your eyes again? Wouldn't it be great to have dinner in a restaurant with somebody and not know absolutely in advance what they were going to order?

KATY
(*Can't take it any longer*)
Look, if I thought that way, I wouldn't tell you about it. I would have the good sense to keep my mouth shut. Why don't you? Why do you have to burden me with this information?

JEFF
Because you asked me.

KATY
"Because you asked me" is the magic phrase that turns out to be the excuse for every stupid thing you ever told me. Because I ask you is why you tell me the roast beef is too done. Because I *ask* you is why you tell me my new dress is too tight. Has it ever occurred to you that you might lie once in a while? And you might stop telling me things I don't want to hear whether I ask you or whether I don't ask you!

JEFF
Well, welcome back. I've missed you.

KATY
What do you mean?

45

JEFF

Well, I wasn't at all comfortable with you playing the Earth Mother—knowing all and understanding all.

KATY

But it didn't work out the way I expected. I thought you had a confession to make. I thought you were going to be rueful and penitent. And I was going to be forgiving. The reason I can't be understanding is that there is nothing to understand except that you have started to ogle teenyboppers in your seminar!

JEFF

Elsie is a graduate student. She has to be at least twenty-two.

KATY

Oh, give me *all* the details! What size shoe does she take? How does she like her eggs?

JEFF

Never mind that—I haven't told you my problem.

KATY

But I know your problem! Your problem is how to extricate yourself from (a) your depressing job, (b) your depressing wife, and (c) your depressing children so you will be free to go off on a bicycle tour with Chuckles, the laughing girl!

JEFF

I thought you were too intelligent to say a thing like that.

46

KATY

But I'm not, I'm absolutely not. How come you haven't noticed that?

JEFF

Katy—

KATY

Your standard method for calming me down on all occasions is to tell me how intelligent I am. It's a kind of blackmail, and it's idiotic besides. Sometimes it's proper to lose your temper. Do you know it's the first sign of mental illness when you don't respond appropriately?

JEFF

Okay, you're not mental. Now, listen for one minute. My problem is I don't know whether or not to pass this girl.

KATY

Have I heard you correctly? Your problem is *what?*

JEFF

(*Going ahead on his own*)

Well, her paper on *The Waste Land* came in yesterday, and it's simply not graduate work. She doesn't even know what a nonrestrictive clause is.

KATY

(*Feigning horror*)

Oh, no, you're jesting! She doesn't know a nonrestrictive clause? Where has she been? I don't like the sound of this at all. And I'm afraid this little romance will never come to flower.

JEFF

(*Interrupting*)

Are you going to go on and on? Or are you going to try and see the point?

KATY

Okay, you have to flunk her. Flunk her.

JEFF

Yes, but you see what that will mean?

KATY

What?

JEFF

She will have to repeat the course.

KATY

Let her repeat it.

JEFF

But I don't want her back in my seminar all next semester.

KATY

You don't? Oh, it's because of all those clauses.

JEFF

(*Angry himself now*)

Don't you see! I want to get her out of my class! I want to get her out of my mind! I want to get her out of my subconscious!

KATY

Oh?

48

JEFF

Listen, if I could press a button that would put her safely in Alaska, I would do it! Oh, boy, would I! I'm not Kevin, for God's sake, I can't be mooning over schoolgirls.

KATY

I see. You mean to be virtuous about this.

JEFF

I mean to do what I am obligated to do.

KATY

I see.

JEFF

Stop saying "I see." You don't see one damn thing! I think I'm going to strangle and you don't even care!
    (JEFF *slams out the front door.*
    KATY *barely has time to change her*
    expression before HE *is back in*)

KATY

My God! Don't tell me there's a sequel.

JEFF

    (*Ignoring that*)
That call was a telegram from Steve. He's coming home for the weekend and he's bringing Phil with him.

KATY

Phil who?

JEFF

Phil-who-does-it-matter? We never got Joe's last name, or Tom's, or—

49

KATY

We do know Joe's last name. It's Carmine and he lives in room fourteen, Adams House. And the reason I know all that is because I had to mail back his damn tennis racquet.

JEFF

Look, I told you. They'll be here for dinner tonight, but we don't have to meet them at the station because they are coming in Phil's car. You got all that?
(JEFF *slams out again*)

KATY

(*Alone*)
I've got all that.
(*Bitterly*)
I've got *everything*. Now watch it. You're not going to be sorry for yourself. But I *am* sorry for myself. All the time! The stock market goes down and I'm sorry for myself. We don't even own one little stock and I'm sorry for myself. But who could have expected True Confessions? And at breakfast, for God's sake! And this was such an absolutely ordinary day. I bet that's what people say after earthquakes. It started out just an ordinary day, a usual day, and then, there you are, poking around in the wreckage looking for the coffee pot.

FRED

(*Entering from the den*)
Is that you, just you? I thought it was a ladies' bridge luncheon.

KATY

It's just me.

FRED

Have you always talked to yourself?

KATY

Yes. It's because I was an only child.

FRED

An only child? I *met* two of your brothers.

KATY

Oh, damn, I forgot that. And it's such a good explanation.

FRED

(*Dropping comfortably onto the
sofa*)

Well, peace, heavenly peace—with loved ones far away!

KATY

(*Trying to appear normal*)
I've got to do the dishes.

FRED

You can't work now. You've got company.

KATY

Oh, Fred, you're not company. And the longer I leave those dishes, the stickier they get.
(*We hear an edge in her voice which,
as* SHE *goes on, is only barely con-
trolled hysteria*)

It has been explained to me that if I soaked those dishes in cold water for five minutes, they'd be easier. But will I soak them? Not on your life. Far be it from me to do anything the easy way. Never let it be said that I was systematic. God forbid. Do you suppose if I had a dishwasher it would enrich my life? Do you suppose that if out in that kitchen I had a white Hotpoint chugging away, I would find true happiness? It is most unlikely. The truth of the matter is that I am insatiable.

(*Now really close to tears*)

Oh, Fred, I don't know. I just don't know. I really don't know.

FRED

You need a drink.

(*Gets up to fix one*)

KATY

At ten o'clock in the morning?

FRED

I haven't checked the hour, but you need a drink.

KATY

I can't drink after breakfast. That's depraved.

FRED

Sure you can.

(*Hands one to her*)

And you won't be struck by a bolt of lightning. I've already checked that out.

KATY

Fred, would you believe that Jeff has fallen in love with a girl in his class?

FRED

Sure.

KATY

You mean he's *discussed* it with you?

FRED

Certainly not. But he had a lot to say about the deplorable state of the cups and saucers around here. I was able to arrive at another conclusion.

KATY

Oh, he mentioned the cups, did he?
          (*Suddenly desperate*)
Oh, Fred, honey—what am I going to do?

FRED

Well, what *is* the situation? He's sleeping with her? He's having an affair with her? He's moving out? What?

KATY

It's worse than that. Much worse than that. He's not sleeping with her. He's not having an affair with her. He just *yearns* after her.
          (FRED *smiles, and* KATY *reacts with
          near tears again*)
Are you laughing? Because there's not one thing funny about it, not one goddamn thing!

FRED

(*Trying to give her a friendly pat*)

Oh, come on, now.

KATY

(*Jumping away*)

Don't you "oh, come on, now" me! And I swear to God if you say one word about mountains and molehills I will strike you with that andiron.

FRED

Katy dear, I love you and you know I love you. And I would be happy to have your wet tears on my strong shoulder. But I honestly don't understand what is so earth-shaking about this.

KATY

Okay, listen to me. I could stand it if I learned that he was sleeping with every third girl in that rotten class.

FRED

It's a good class.

KATY

(*Paying no attention, going right on*)

I wouldn't like it. I'd hate it. But I could deal with it. I could cope with it. I'd tell myself it was middle age, animal instinct, male menopause. But it would be a thing *done* and it would be separate from me—or I could try and keep it separate from me. But when he sits on the edge of our bed at four o'clock in the morning and taps cigarette ashes into his shoes and stares into space because he is daydreaming about somebody else—that's a *betrayal*. We have a relationship and, damnit, his subconscious belongs to me!

(*The wind has now gone out of her*)

Maybe I should talk to a lawyer.

FRED

Talk to me.

KATY

My God, I keep forgetting you're a lawyer.

FRED

That's how I happen to be teaching in law school. Obviously you don't want a divorce.

KATY

Is that so obvious?

FRED

(HE *is not taking this seriously;* HE *is just trying to calm her down*)

As I see it, in your present mood you'd take him for every cent he's got except that he hasn't got a cent.

KATY

Hell, if he had a cent, I wouldn't want it.

FRED

To be totally realistic, how would you estimate your estate?

KATY

Estate? You mean this *house?* It's mortgaged for more than we could ever sell it for!

55

FRED

You have no savings account?

KATY

Not really. There's this little account of six hundred dollars that we always kept for medical expense in case I got pregnant again. You see, we always hoped we'd have a girl.

(*Her voice breaks*)

FRED

(*Stopping what* HE *fears may be new tears*)

Look, Katy, if you want to lapse into pathos, you will have to do it on your own time. I will not be a party to it. But if you want a little free advice, I'll give it to you.

KATY

Okay, I want it. I *think*.

FRED

Urge Jeff to have a little fling with this girl.

KATY

(*Stares at him a second*)

Quite apart from the fact that that is a disgusting idea, how would I go about it?

(*Assuming another, wifely voice*)

"Jeff, honey, after you're through school today, would you stop at Gristede's and pick up two quarts of milk! And oh, if you should have time left over, why don't you and Elsie have a fling? I have already rented a room at the Bedford Motel under the name of Edison. Thomas B. Edison."

56

FRED

Oh, it's Elsie.

KATY

You know Elsie?

FRED

Yes, she's in one of *my* classes.

KATY

So tell me about her!

FRED

Well, she's not overwhelmingly bright.

KATY

On that point, word has reached me.

FRED

But she's a nice girl.

KATY

Fred, I've got a hell of a good idea. You have a fling with
Elsie. It will solve everybody's problems.

FRED

I think you should decide how you're going to play this
part. You are tough and sardonic, or an open, bleeding
heart? Which is it?

KATY

(*Subsiding*)

Fred, it just hit. I haven't had time to think.

FRED

I'm taking that into consideration. Nevertheless, I tell you this. There is a way to give Jeff a feeling that he's got a green light here. Find it, do it.

KATY

But why, why, why?

FRED

You can't stand this ambiguous situation. You want a *fait accompli*. Get it.

KATY

(*Sarcastically*)
You think it will clear the air.

FRED

I am thinking of Jeff's shoes. I think he should stop tapping ashes into them—in the middle of the night.

KATY

Never mind what *I* think, what makes *you* think this girl —this Elsie—would conceivably be a party to this horrid little plan?

FRED

Your use of the word "horrid" is very revealing. What's horrid about it? He's an attractive man, she's an attractive girl—

KATY

Fred, I don't think I want to talk to you any more.

FRED

All right, you don't have to. But there's something you ought to know. Things have changed a little since you graduated from Marymount in nineteen hundred and five.

KATY

Six. Nineteen hundred and six.

FRED

Young people today don't have the hangups we used to have.

KATY

By hangups you mean morals?

FRED

I mean they are easier and freer in their relationships. If they feel an attraction, they don't feel they have to wait for bell, book, and candle.

KATY

Just the pill.

FRED

Don't you think you're a little intolerant?

KATY

I think I'm *very* intolerant and I mean to stay that way. If these kids want to jump in and out of the sack like a bunch of Playboy rabbits—

FRED

(*Interrupting*)

Bunnies. Playboy bunnies. At least get the terminology correct.

KATY

Actually, I blame their parents. If they were brought up to believe in God and right and wrong, they wouldn't be so screwed up.

FRED

Did you say screwed up?

KATY

Is that phrase incorrect also?

FRED

No, it's totally precise. I just never heard you use it before.

KATY

That's because you're getting me mad.

FRED

Get madder. It circulates the blood and is good for the complexion. Give me your hand.

KATY

For what?

FRED

For one minute.

KATY

You're drunk.

FRED

On one scotch? Give me your hand.

KATY
(Very tentatively doing so)
All right, you have my hand.

FRED

(HE *holds her hand lightly*)
Now I want your attention.

KATY

My hand is clammy. From holding the glass.

FRED

Yes, so is mine.

KATY

Fred, this is crazy!
(*Starts to pull her hand away*)

FRED

(*Holding onto it*)
Wait, wait, wait—this won't take a minute.
(HE *gently places his other hand on
hers so that* HE *now has her hand
between the two of his.* HE *gently
massages her wrist with his fingers.*
KATY *is slightly mesmerized*)
Now. Is that disagreeable?

KATY

(SHE *is going to be honest even if it's
embarrassing*)
No, it isn't. But what is the point?

FRED

I wanted you to notice something. *That* was contact. And
contact is pleasant.

KATY

(*Irked and feeling a little foolish*)

My God, you're turning into an encounter group!

FRED

And you're the last of the Latter-day Saints. But I don't think your case is hopeless.

KATY

I don't know what the hell you are talking about.

FRED

But you do. That's why that little blue vein in your neck is throbbing. So any time you want that second lesson in the beginner's course, you have but to call me. Remember, I am within easy walking distance.

KATY

That'll be the day.

FRED

The evening is actually more convenient for me.

KATY

Oh, go to hell. Go home.

FRED

Going, going—oh, wait. To change the subject. Miss Elsie will be dropping in at my place later.

KATY

(*Drawing false conclusions*)

Oh, really?

There's no need for the "oh" or the "really." Her term paper is overdue and she's dropping it off around five o'clock.

KATY

So?

FRED

I thought maybe, all things considered, you'd like to meet her.

KATY

No, no, no, no.
(*Without a break*)
Yes, I would. I would like to see those damn even teeth. But I'm not going to go over there.

FRED

She can come over here.

KATY

You mean you'll tell her that there's a crazy lady who wants to look in her mouth.

FRED

You have no head for intrigue. You'll have to learn. I'll give her a book and ask her to return it to you. Trust me.

KATY

Up until this morning, I always did trust you.

63

FRED

And that has changed a little. Good. The morning hasn't been lost at all.

> (HE *leaves*)

KATY

> (*To herself*)

I shall "take arms against a sea of troubles and by opposing end them." And I know just where I can start.

> (KATY *picks up the hammer Hughie*
> *has left and starts smashing the*
> *teacups, one by one*)

CURTAIN

Act Two

*Late afternoon the same day. Terrace
doors are wide open.* KATY *is sitting
in a chair right of sofa, folding
napkins.*

JEFF

(Calling offstage)

Katy!

*(*KATY *rises and hurries out to the
terrace.*

Entering, looking for KATY*)*

Katy!

*(*JEFF *goes into the kitchen.*

KATY *enters from the terrace)*

I know what I should do about Jeff. I should retreat into an icy silence. Oh, hell, with a whole house full of people who would notice an icy silence? But one thing I will not do. I will not ask him if he saw her today.

(JEFF *comes in from the kitchen*)

JEFF

Hi. Was there a letter—was there anything from Dean Dennis?

KATY

No. Do you think that means you're not going to get it?

JEFF

I think it means I haven't heard.

KATY

Well, did you see her today?

JEFF

No. I didn't meet my poetry seminar today.

KATY

What did you do?

JEFF

Nothing.

KATY

You mean you spent the day just avoiding Elsie? I think that's . . .

JEFF

Katy, I want to apologize for my silly outburst this morning.

KATY

(*Catching herself up and trying her
icy silence now*)

Let's not talk about it.

JEFF

But you brought it up!

KATY

I know I did! And that's very inconsistent of me. But we must face up to the fact that I happen to be very inconsistent!

JEFF

(*A bit desperate*)

It's just that I am used to confiding in you.

KATY

Let's not talk about it.

JEFF

I thought if I could put it into words, I could put it out of my head.

KATY

One more syllable and I will leave the room!

JEFF

I only want to say that I am sorry and I wish that—
(KATY *starts to leave the room*)

Okay, we won't talk about it.
>   (*An effort to change the subject*)
I gather we are going to eat outside.

KATY

I find it easier to deal with strangers in the open air. There are so many distractions, like slapping away mosquitoes and keeping the candles lit.

JEFF

Strangers? You mean that kid who's coming? Don't tell me you're letting yourself get fussed about him. You should be glad the boys feel free to bring their friends home.

KATY

The next time *you* be the one that makes a fancy dessert and finds the clean sheets and I'll be the one that's glad. Do you know that one time when Madame Chiang Kai-shek visited the White House she brought her own satin sheets—and Eleanor Roosevelt was furious? I wouldn't be furious, I'd be thrilled!

JEFF

What kind of a crazy tablecloth is this? What are these things all over it?

KATY

Easter bunnies and jelly beans.

JEFF

For Memorial Day?

KATY

Your brother gave us that cloth four years ago. And it's the only one we have big enough for this table.

JEFF

Of course, it will look fine once we put on the Santa Claus mugs.

KATY

Never mind the cloth. Just promise that tonight you will talk to this kid.

JEFF

I always talk to them.

KATY

The hell you do. You say, "And how do you like Harvard?" and he says, "It's okay, I guess," and the rest is silence.

JEFF

I never notice any silence.

KATY

That's because I jabber away about the Knicks and the Jets, where I beguile one and all by my total ignorance of the subject.

JEFF

Look, Fred is alone over there. He hasn't been lost for a word since the night he saw *Carnal Knowledge*. Let's invite him over.

71

KEVIN

(*Coming from school, through the terrace*)

Hey, we're going to eat outside! That's great!

KATY

I thought you had a meeting. I thought we were going to leave little dried-up things in the oven.

KEVIN

I heard that Phil was coming home with Steve. So I got out of it.

JEFF

Good. Welcome aboard.

KATY

Welcome and one other thing. I have been up in your room trying to face the facts of life. How you can have seven jackets on the floor when I know for certain that you only own two jackets is a mystery I am not even going to pursue.

KEVIN

But you are going to pursue something.

KATY

Right. You're the one who keeps lecturing us all on ecology and the pollution problem.

KEVIN

That's right. Yeah.

72

Well, under your bed there appears to be about eleven bottles—Coke, root beer, beer, Diet-Rite, Fresca. I would call it a pollution area. If you want to do your little bit for the environment, I suggest you recycle them the hell out of there.

KEVIN

(Interrupting hastily, heading for the stairs. At the same time we hear the sound of a car on the driveway outside)

Okay, okay. I'll do it right now.
(KEVIN vanishes upstairs)

JEFF

(At the indoor edge of the terrace)

A car just came in the driveway. I suppose it's Steve and his friend.

KATY

Or it could be the plumber. It's one week since I called him about our bathtub—which does not drain. How come you haven't noticed that it doesn't drain?

JEFF

Because I never look back.
(HUGHIE dashes in from terrace door)

HUGHIE

Boy, is Phil ever gorgeous! I mean, out of sight!
(HUGHIE dashes right out again)

73

KATY

(*Blank look at* JEFF)
Phil is gorgeous? Is he trying to tell us something?

JEFF

(*With a shrug*)
I suppose Phil's hair is *really* long.

KATY

Don't be silly. All their hair is really long.

JEFF

Okay, then, he's brought home a member of the Gay Lib.
We shall just have to be brave.

KATY

You don't suppose Stevie has become a—?

JEFF

A homosexual? Yes, that's what I do suppose. I suppose
that in due time all three of them will become homo-
sexuals. Remember, we have the perfect breeding ground
here. The Aggressive Mother, the Absent Father. It all fits.
But tell yourself this. At least we won't have to cope
with grandchildren. Think of the relief that will be! And
pretty soon, maybe in twenty or thirty years, these kids
will stop coming home altogether. As I see it, the day will
dawn when we will have licked, entirely licked, the clean
sheet problem!

> (STEVE *enters with a ravishing-*
> *looking* GIRL. STEVE *is a Harvard sen-*
> *ior.* HE *has obviously made some ef-*

74

fort to look halfway conventional for his PARENTS; *God knows what* HE *looks like at Harvard. The* GIRL, PHIL, *is* FELICIA ANDRAYSON, *about twenty-six, extremely pretty in a theatrical way.* HUGHIE *is close at* FELICIA'S *heels*)

STEVE

Hi, Dad. Hi, Mom.
(KATY *just stares at* STEVE *and* FELICIA)

STEVE

(*To his* MOTHER)
Don't just stand there. Look—a tie
(*Rubbing his cheek*)
—no beard. And I got my hair cut just for you. So give me one of your better-grade hugs.
(HE *hugs her and* SHE *responds*)
Okay, that's better. Love you six.
(*This last phrase is thrown away*)
Now I want you both to meet Phil—

FELICIA

It's Felicia. Felicia Andrayson. How do you do? Thank you for letting me come. I'll try not to be in the way.

JEFF

Miss Andrayson.
(THEY *shake hands*)

75

FELICIA

This house is marvelous. It's just like the stage setting for *A Long Day's Journey Into Night.*

KATY

Yes, I've always felt that.

FELICIA
(Realizing it didn't come out quite right)

Oh, I don't mean the New York production! I never saw that. But it was done at Stockbridge last summer. And the room gave you the same feeling—you know—sort of stark but fascinating.
(Suddenly remembering)
Oh, I've got to get something out of the car!

STEVE

I'll get it.

FELICIA

No, you'd never find it. It's under a lot of junk.

HUGHIE

I'll come. You may need me.
(FELICIA goes out through terrace followed by HUGHIE)

JEFF
(Quickly calling after)
I'll move *my* car and you can get closer.
(JEFF goes. STEVE is left alone with KATY)

STEVE

Well, what do you think of Phil?

KATY

I'd say, stark but fascinating.

STEVE

Oh, that. She meant that to be a compliment.

KATY

We both did.

STEVE

Mom, do me a favor. Please don't ask her what her father does.

KATY

Is it a big secret or something?

STEVE

No, it just sounds so creepy. It sounds as though you were really asking, "Is your family respectable enough for our little boy to play with?"

KATY

Okay, I get the message. Is it all right if I ask what *she* does?

STEVE

She's an actress.

KATY

That figures. How old is she?

STEVE

Twenty-six.

KATY

You mean—?

STEVE

That's right. When I'm a hundred, she's going to be a hundred and four.

> (HE's *been studying her, and now*
> *changes his tone to something inti-*
> *mate and friendly;* THEY'VE *always*
> *had a fond relationship*)

Hey, sunshine. What's the matter?

KATY

Why do you think something's the matter?

STEVE

Because we've met before and I know the storm signals. Your eyes are too blue and you've got two cigarettes burning besides the one in your hand. At first I thought it was all Oedipal, that you were worried I was leaving you for a younger woman. But it's not that.

KATY

You're sure?

STEVE

What did happen? Where's the old twinkle that used to make you look at least three months younger? Did you lose an inlay? I know what it is, you just learned about Gloria Steinem and realize you've wasted your life. You should have been a bricklayer.

KATY

(Relenting and smiling)

Oh, Stevie, you're as crazy as ever.

STEVE

But you're not as sane as ever. You used to find me irresistible.

KATY

Oh, I did, did I? What makes you so sure?

STEVE

Because after you made scrambled eggs for everybody, you'd make me poached.

KATY

Well, you used to bring me Walnettos home from school. Stevie, look. I am upset. This program has just been interrupted for a number of important announcements. All of them most unwelcome. And I have the feeling you are on the verge of making another announcement.

STEVE

Like what?

KATY

Like you're getting married.

STEVE

Are you kidding? Mom. I don't plan to get married until I am forty-seven. If then.

KATY

I see. And what is so special about being forty-seven?

STEVE

That's when most men have their first coronaries. I may need somebody to take care of me. Or maybe you'll get yourself in great physical shape and be there at my bedside with those tasty low-cholesterol meals that only you—

KATY

Stop it! Don't talk that way. I can't *bear* to hear you sound so cynical.

STEVE

Okay, I won't talk that way.
(*Puts his arm around her*)
But what's happened to your sense of humor?

KATY

God knows. I swear I had it as recently as yesterday. Well, what does Felicia think about your airy views on the subject of marriage?

STEVE

She agrees with me totally. She was married once and she's sworn off forever. She doesn't think marriage is viable in this century.

KATY

I should never have a drink at ten o'clock in the morning.
(JEFF, FELICIA, *and* HUGHIE *return from the car,* HUGHIE *carrying a large suitcase and* JEFF *carrying a smaller one.* FELICIA *herself has a large bag of vegetables in her arms*)

FELICIA

(*Smiling at* HUGHIE)

Hughie is really strong, because that's a heavy suitcase.

HUGHIE

I practice with weights.

FELICIA

I could tell that.

KATY

(*To* HUGHIE)

You go get out of those school clothes.

HUGHIE

(*Bounding up the stairs*)

Be right back, Phil!

FELICIA

(*Referring to the bag in her arms*)

Does it matter where I put this?

KATY

I'll take it.

(SHE *does, starting for the kitchen*)

FELICIA

It's just corn and tomatoes. Steve said you liked sweet
corn—

KATY

Thank you, I do like sweet corn.

FELICIA

Actually this corn was flown in from Florida so I promise you nothing.

KATY

Oh, why not?

STEVE

You know that they say corn should be eaten within hours after it is picked. If not minutes. Otherwise sugar turns into carbohydrates or something ghastly.

(*The conversation is now among the* OTHERS, *but* KATY *still stands at the kitchen door listening to it*)

FELICA

As I see it, the only way to get a decent ear of corn is to take a kettle of boiling water out into the field, pour it over the corn while it's growing, and then get down on your hands and knees and munch right there.

(*To* JEFF, *abruptly*)

Do you think I sound affected?

JEFF

Not at all. Why?

FELICIA

Because a lot of people do. I've had all this voice work. Two drama schools and three rep companies.

(SHE *pronounces the words carefully*)

And now when I start to talk, I see people looking heavenward, as though they'd got struck with Ophelia at breakfast.

JEFF
(*Examining the stickers of* FELICIA's
bag)

The French Line, the Italian Line, Cunard—you've been a lot of places.

FELICIA

No, that's my father's bag. He's been a lot of places.

KATY
(*To* STEVE)

It's okay, I won't ask.

FELICIA

Fortune magazine says he is the eighth richest man in the United States.

JEFF

What does he do?

FELICIA

He used to manufacture electronics. Now he just manufactures money.

KATY

You sound disapproving. I gather you are not close to your father.

FELICIA

Well, he divorced my mother—or, anyway, they got divorced—when I was eighteen months old. And I didn't see him again until Mother died—that was in California. And somebody, I forget who, put me on a plane for New York with a tag around my neck. I mean a real baggage tag with my name printed on it—and my destination. I was furious because, while I wasn't quite five, I did know my name and where I was going. When the plane landed this man met me. He was very tan with lots of curly white hair. And he laughed and threw me in the air and hugged me. It was Eddie, the chauffeur, and for years he was my best friend. Eventually, I saw my father, but he sent me right off to rattle around in a great big school.

STEVE

I didn't know you were still bitter about that.

FELICIA

I'm not. I'm neutral. He's very generous with me. Let's say that he's the friend I've got at Chase Manhattan.
> (HUGHIE *hurries downstairs, having changed his shirt*)

HUGHIE

Hey, Phil, do you want to hear a neat riddle?

FELICIA

Sure, I love riddles.
> (KATY *takes this opportunity to get to the kitchen*)

HUGHIE

If April showers bring May flowers, what do May flowers bring?

FELICIA

I give up. What do May flowers bring?

HUGHIE

Pilgrims.

> (KEVIN *reappears from upstairs, his*
> *arms filled with an unbelievable*
> *number of bottles*)

KEVIN

Phil! Hello, there! Can you see me under the bottles?

FELICIA

> (As KEVIN *tries to stick out a hand in*
> *greeting, which is impossible*)

Hi, Kevin, sure! We'll shake hands later. How's everything with you? Still got that drunken math teacher?

KEVIN

Oh, Carter. He went into analysis and sobered up. He talks about nothing but his stupid analyst so we aren't learning any math, but at least he doesn't throw up in the wastebasket any more.

> (KEVIN *goes to the kitchen with the*
> *bottles*)

HUGHIE

Hey, Phil, do you want to come up and see my fish tank?

FELICIA

> (*With a smile at the* OTHERS *over*
> HUGHIE's *sudden and obvious infatu-*
> *ation*)

I'd love to, Hughie.

STEVE

To go into that room you need a surgical mask.
(KATY *returns from the kitchen as*
HUGHIE *and* FELICIA *are going up the*
stairs)

HUGHIE

Phil, do you know what one strawberry said to the other
strawberry?

FELICIA

Nope. What did one strawberry say to the other strawberry?

HUGHIE

If you weren't so fresh we wouldn't be in this jam!
(FELICIA *pats his head as* SHE *and*
HUGHIE *disappear upstairs.* KEVIN *re-*
turns from the kitchen)

JEFF

(*Once* FELICIA *is gone*)
What a charming girl.

KATY

Yes. Stevie, look, you can put Felicia in your room. The
sheets are clean. And then you can move in with Kevin.

KEVIN

Why does he have to move in with me?

JEFF

Now, that shouldn't require great deliberation.

KEVIN

But I've got a term paper to finish! I've got to be able to concentrate.

KATY

I don't see why Stevie should interfere with your concentration.

KEVIN

Phil sleeps in his room at Cambridge, why can't she sleep with him here?
>   (*There is a profound silence*)
Steve, I just didn't think. I'm sorry.

STEVE

It's not enough to be sorry. Go kill yourself.
>   (*There is more silence.* KEVIN *goes to
>   the kitchen*)
Well, I guess the cat is out of the bag.

KATY

But the cat has been in the bag, right?

JEFF

>   (*With authority*)
Katy, we are not going to conduct this discussion on that level. It is demeaning to all of us.

KATY

>   (*Penitent*)
I know. I apologize.

JEFF

However, Steve, there is something I must say.

STEVE

You're going to say that you know I am over twenty-one and that I am free to lead my own life any way I choose. And you are prepared to be tolerant if and when—

JEFF
(*Interrupting sharply*)
I'm not going to say that. I am, by God, not going to say that. That was last year's speech. I'm going to say something else. Your mother and I are over forty. And we think we should be free to lead our life the way *we* choose. And we think you should be prepared to be tolerant if and when we decide to conduct our lives and our house the way we have always conducted it.

STEVE

So who's asking you to change?

KATY

This girl is your mistress and you're bringing her home. That's asking *something*, isn't it?

STEVE

What? Just tell me what?

KATY

Well, you are asking us to countenance—what we don't wish to countenance.

STEVE

Countenance? My God, do people still use that word?

JEFF

It would appear so.

STEVE

I think you both are being damned unfair. I had no plan whatsoever to conduct my liaison—I'm sure that's the word you would use, Mom—I had no intention of conducting my liaison in the chaste environs of your house. I assure you that Phil will be able to keep her hands off me during the brief period that we are, quote, under your roof, unquote!

JEFF

Okay, okay.

STEVE

Furthermore, you never would have known at all if Kevin could ever learn to keep his stupid mouth shut.

KATY

And that's another thing! Why would you scandalize Kevin by telling him about it?

STEVE

There are two answers to that question. In the first place, I didn't tell Kevin. He just found out when he was in Cambridge. In the second place, *nothing* scandalizes Kevin.

KATY

You mean he's sleeping around, too?

STEVE

Probably not. He's too shy. But more than half of his friends are.

JEFF

(*Standing, with sweeping gestures*)
Well, folks, I'm afraid that's all we have time for. But I want to thank you all for being here—

KATY

What's got into you?

JEFF

(*Heading for the liquor*)
An Excedrin headache. I'm going to take something for it, and *not* Excedrin!
(*Pouring himself a drink*)

STEVE

I'm sorry about that, Dad.

JEFF

You don't have to be sorry. At least one thing has been clarified for me. When we say that you are free to do what you want, we really mean that you are free to do what we want you to do. I need to think about that.
(*Goes to his office, taking the drink with him and closing the door*)

STEVE

(*Uncomfortable, but resuming his natural brightness in an effort to change the subject*)

90

What can I do about dinner? Is there anything that needs to be scraped or peeled or chopped?

KATY

(*Distracted, looking at* JEFF's *door*)
Thank you, Steve, but it's all ready.

STEVE

What is it?

KATY

The recipe that I tore out of the *Standard Star* said "Pot Roast With a Difference." Actually, the only difference I could find is that you punch cloves into the raw onions. I must say that I felt very adventurous pushing cloves into the onions.

STEVE

Mom, are you still upset?
(*Pause*)
About me and Phil?

KATY

I am not thinking about it.

STEVE

Honestly, it's no big deal.

KATY

I gather that. Stevie, I want to ask you a question.

STEVE

You want to know if I'm smoking pot, dropping acid, taking speed—

KATY

Stevie, do you ever go to church any more?

STEVE

Not really.

KATY

What do you mean, not really?

STEVE

I mean, no, I don't. I find I don't get anything out of it.

KATY

What did you expect to get out of it—a good tan?

STEVE

It's just so empty. Those bored people, those nothing sermons. Hell, I can feel closer to God walking in the woods.

KATY

And how often do you walk in the woods? You know, one of these days I'm going to meet somebody who tells me he feels closer to God in Schrafft's.

STEVE

That's because of the service.

KATY

Why are you so flippant?

STEVE

Mom, I have to be *something*—and you're not leaving me any room.

KATY

I take it, then, that you don't believe in anything.

STEVE

I didn't say that. I guess I believe in a God, some kind of a God. I certainly don't believe in a hereafter.

KATY

Then what's the point of believing in God? That's like saying you think success is important but you don't want the money.

STEVE

Now who's flippant? Look, Mom, you made us go to church just the way you made us get polio shots—to be on the safe side.

KATY

I think that's a fair enough way to put it.

STEVE

Just tell yourself it didn't take.

KATY

You never got polio.

STEVE

Mom, I'm not blaming you. I even understand. When I was a little boy you tried to protect me from sharp knives and rusty nails and high rocks—and now you want to protect me from life. I don't want to be protected from life. I want to live it.

And then what?

And then who cares? I know you have total certainty that if you toe the line, contribute to UNICEF, and send over casseroles to the neighbors when they have the flu, choirs of angels will bear you happily to fields of bliss—

Oh, crap.

(*Pretended shock*)

Oh, Mother!

Damnit, I am not as simple-minded as that. Forget what *I* think. Let's go with Pascal for a minute.

The fifty-fifty bit.

That's right. If there is a fifty-fifty chance of immortality, why not play it with the believers? Remember, nobody has ever seriously questioned those odds. Nobody has ever suggested that it was an eighty-twenty proposition.

So what does all that mean to you?

I think you should impose standards and disciplines on

94

yourself so that you might just possibly slip into eternity with Thomas More instead of going to hell with Hitler.

STEVE

You would condemn Adolf Hitler to hell for all eternity?

KATY

You're damn right I would! You wouldn't?

STEVE

I don't ever make sweeping judgments.

KATY

You don't? Well, try it sometime. It can be very satisfying.

STEVE

I just don't have your total certainty about every single thing in the universe.

KATY

I'll tell you something. My total certainties hit a land mine about ten o'clock this morning. And no. I have no plan to explain that remark. Now, go get dressed.

STEVE

I am dressed.

KATY

Then get undressed.

STEVE

(*Huffy*)
No need to be clearer. I'll go.

CENTER

KATY

Don't be dramatic. I mean just a few minutes. I want to count to a hundred by sevens. I will find it stabilizing if I can still do it.

(STEVE *goes upstairs*)

Seven, fourteen, twenty-one, twenty-eight, thirty-five, forty-two—I should be much younger or much older. If I were twenty years older, these would be my grandchildren and I could blame their parents for the way they were turning out. And if I were twenty years younger, they'd be infants and I could give them orange-flavored aspirin and put them to bed. Now they can go to bed by themselves—if only they would!

(JEFF *emerges from his den*)

JEFF

You never seem to run out of things to say to yourself.

KATY

It's okay, I'm a good listener. You know, I have the definite feeling this day is going to get worse.

JEFF

It won't be easy, but maybe we can swing it.

KATY

Do you suppose *Hughie* has ever had an affair?

JEFF

What?

KATY

Well, he's been ten minutes up in that room with Felicia—

JEFF

What I really want is another drink, but I suppose I could switch to coffee. Is there some coffee on?

(*Starting for the kitchen*)

KATY

There's coffee but there's no cups. I smashed them with a hammer.

JEFF

(*Turning*)

You—

KATY

Smashed them with a hammer. You heard me.

JEFF

(*A sigh*)

I'm not even going to ask about it. But what am I supposed to put the coffee in—a glass?

KATY

There are the Santa mugs.

JEFF

Peachy. Do you want some coffee?

KATY

I guess so.

(KEVIN *comes out of the kitchen, quickly sidestepping his* FATHER, *who goes after coffee;* HE *stands embarrassed*)

KEVIN

Mom, I feel like the world's prize idiot.

KATY

You are the world's prize idiot. By the way, what is your attitude toward this whole thing?

KEVIN

What whole thing?

KATY

All these boys and girls casually sleeping around.

KEVIN

Mom, I don't know what my attitude is. If I knew I probably wouldn't tell you. But I honestly don't know.

KATY

Okay. Would you please sweep up the terrace? There's a broom out there.

> (JEFF *enters from kitchen, staring at the two Santa mugs, filled with coffee,* HE *has in his hands*)

JEFF

These things are revolting.

> (KEVIN *is gone*)

KATY

> (*Getting back to what is really on her mind*)

We should never have sent Stevie to Harvard.

JEFF

We didn't send him to Harvard. We couldn't afford to send him to Harvard. He got that scholarship and those two jobs all on his own. And he's a good student and basically a good kid.

KATY

I love the way you use the word "basically," meaning something wrong has happened. "He's an ax murderer but basically he's a real doll."

JEFF

And I love the way you jump to ax murderer as soon as you hear the word "sex."

KATY

Jeff, please let's not quarrel. I just don't have the energy. The man that came about the washer yesterday said it needed a whole new unit. That's what I need, a whole new unit. Oh, God, I wish it was nineteen forty-eight!

JEFF

What was so special about nineteen forty-eight?

KATY

We were in college and the whole world was possible and nobody talked about saving the environment because the environment was just great. And you could read the paper in the morning without wanting to kill yourself. And since we didn't have television, you couldn't see the seven o'clock news. That was a saving. You never did see people, actual people, shot down in gorgeous living color.

JEFF

(*Gently*)

Katy, we were young in nineteen forty-eight.

KATY

But that was only part of it. People believed in things. And they had standards, or they pretended they had standards. And college kids didn't sleep around.

JEFF

Of course they did.

KATY

Well, we didn't.

JEFF

No, we didn't. Do you suppose we should have been given the Congressional Medal of Honor? Katy, you think the way you were brought up is not only the right way but the only way.

KATY

That's not true.

JEFF

The hell it isn't. Other women your age—

KATY

I will listen to nothing that begins with the phrase "Other women your age!"

JEFF

Okay, other women read Suzy's column or whoever's column, and when they learn what all the glamorous people are doing and saying in Acapulco, they feel twinges of envy. You feel twinges of righteousness.

KATY

I do not.

JEFF

Oh, but you do! Katy, there is something you just will not face. I think it's time you did face it.

KATY

Face it? Face what?

JEFF

You think these kids today are not only too free but probably on the road to ruin. Maybe they're not. Maybe by the time they're forty, they will be in better shape than we are.

KATY

You mean all those healthy drugs.

JEFF

Damnit, stay with my point! We've been strict all our lives and look at us. *Look* at us!
        (*Slight pause*)
Something is missing. You know something is missing.

KATY

        (*Painfully*)
Love, maybe.

JEFF

Oh, Katy, you know I love you—

101

(Second thought, and sharper)
—not that you seem to care any more—

KATY

Why do you say that?

JEFF

You know perfectly well that I have only to throw an arm over your pillow, for you to say, "I've just had my hair done." The rest of the time it's "Not tonight, honey, I'm really so sleepy—"

KATY

Sometimes I *am* sleepy—

JEFF

Sometimes!

KATY

You know, a man *will* believe you're too tired to go out to a movie. Why is it that he won't believe—

JEFF

Maybe men are not that interested in movies. Actually, it would be simpler if I didn't love you.

KATY

You mean you'd feel freer to have a trial spin or what Thurber used to call a little "pounce in the clover?"

JEFF

That may have sounded all right from Thurber. From you it sounds downright ghastly. Don't talk about what you don't *know* about.

KATY

Oh, but I've just had a crash course! I know a lot of things I didn't know yesterday. Jeff, I have a proposition to make. Actually, it's not a proposition, it's an ultimatum. I am leaving on Monday.

JEFF

Why don't you take a little nap? You're tired.

KATY

What do I have to do to get you to take me seriously?

JEFF

Talk sense.

KATY

But I am leaving on Monday. I wouldn't go before that because I don't want Steve to think it had anything to do with him or Felicia.

JEFF

You're leaving for where—for what? Do you plan to come back or do you plan to start life anew as a meter maid in Kansas City?

KATY

I plan to come back after you've had your affair.

JEFF

My affair? My affair with who?

KATY

Your affair with Elsie, or maybe she has a friend even fairer than she.

JEFF

If your plan is to drive me nuts you're nicely on the way.

KATY

Jeff, I am not joking.

JEFF

I'm glad to hear that, because you're not at all funny.

KATY

I find I cannot stand the present situation.

JEFF

Which is?

KATY

Which is you with that permanent look of convalescence! It's you with the desperate air of one who has missed the chance, missed the boat, missed the girl! I suggest that life would be more tolerable for all of us if you would find a way to get it out of your system!

JEFF

Get it out of my system? That sounds like a teacher I had in the fifth grade.

KATY

I could be coarser, but then you would be offended.

JEFF

I thought I knew you. After twenty-three years, I really thought I knew you! But if I am following this at all, what you are saying is that what you find absolutely shocking in Stevie's behavior would be just absolutely dandy for me!

KATY

Jeff, please be patient with me. I have stopped making judgments. Because all of them have flown back in my face. I don't know what's right any more. I just know what I can stand. And I can't stand this. I really can't. Oh, I bet if I exercised and took vitamins, I could stand it . . . but I didn't and I don't and I can't!

JEFF

Katy, use your head for a minute. This talk about going someplace. Where could you go? Not to your mother's. She'd think we were getting a divorce and she'd have a nervous breakdown!

KATY

I know that. I'll go visit my brother, Jamie—nobody would ask questions.

JEFF

I'll ask questions. What if I won't put up with it? What if I flatly refuse to let you go?

KATY

And how will you stop me? George C. Scott could handle this with his eyebrows. You couldn't do it with a gun.

JEFF

Okay, I'm a weak sister and I can't even manage my own wife. But I can manage myself.

KATY

You can?

JEFF

I think so. You can stay away ten years and I shall continue, as before, in my dreary, strait-laced way.

KATY

That would be kind of a waste.

JEFF

No doubt. But get this through your head. I may talk like an ass. But I, by God, am not going to behave like one!

KATY

I'll call once in a while and check on that.

JEFF

(*Furious*)
What you need is somebody to give you a good belt!

KATY

(*Maddening*)
But, alas, I don't have anybody.

JEFF

(*Grabbing her by the shoulders*)
Oh, damn you, damn you, anyway!
(STEVE *has started to come down-stairs, stops, embarrassed*)

STEVE

Excuse me, I forgot something upstairs.
(*Turns to go*)

JEFF

Oh, Steve, don't be a goddamn fool! There is no use trying

to be discreet. Your mother and I *were* quarreling. That couldn't be clearer, so let's not bother to pretend.

(*Holding up empty bottle*)

Don't tell me we're out of scotch!

KATY

There's more in the pantry.

(JEFF *bolts to the kitchen*)

STEVE

(*After an uneasy pause*)

I never heard Dad use a tone like that to you.

KATY

For that matter, I never did, either.

STEVE

But why?

KATY

Let's say that I was asking for it.

STEVE

But I don't understand.

KATY

As we said earlier, marriage may not be viable in this century.

STEVE

It is for you and Dad.

KATY

Well, well, well! Now you *have* shocked me! Stevie—you have double standards!

STEVE

(*A bit sheepish*)
Well, you and Dad always seemed so lovey-dovey—

KATY

Well, now we are hawky-talky. Why don't you ring that bell? I think we should start collecting people for dinner.

STEVE

Okay.

> (HE *rings a bell on the desk.* HUGHIE
> *and* FELICIA *are coming downstairs*)

HUGHIE

(*Calling to the* OTHERS)
Phil really liked my fish tank! I'll take the corn, Mom!
> (HE *does, and goes to the kitchen*)

FELICIA

I know I *look* useless, but surely there's something I can do.

KATY

Thank you. There is. You can put these paper plates into the wicker containers. The wicker is supposed to give strength and new magic to the paper plates. I don't believe it, but I play along.

JEFF

> (*Returning from the kitchen with
> a drink in his hand*)
Anybody else want a drink?

STEVE	FELICIA
No, thank you.	No, thank you.

KATY

(*Eying the drink*)

That looks awfully dark. What have you got there, a drink of scotch or a glass of scotch?

JEFF

A glass, my dear. May I get you one?

KATY

No, thank you. And may I suggest that—

JEFF

You may suggest nothing.

KATY

(*Taking a book from the bookshelf
as* HUGHIE *returns from the kitchen
and indicating the terrace*)

Hughie, that table out there is wobbly because one of the legs is short. Stick this book under it.

JEFF

Stick a book under it? A book! Are you crazy?

KATY

(*Looking at the book*)

You told me to throw it out years ago.

JEFF

Why didn't you throw it out? No table leg in the world is three inches short. What we need is a tile. Hughie, there

are some old bathroom tiles in the garage. Get me one.
> (HUGHIE *goes by way of the terrace*)

By the way, the water in that big pot was boiling like crazy, so I turned it off.
> (HE *goes to the terrace even as* KATY
> *is talking*)

KATY

Turned it off! You should have lowered it.
> (*To nobody in particular*)

I wish I knew for certain how long to cook corn. I just leave it in there till I get nervous.
> (KATY *goes to the kitchen.* FELICIA
> *is tucking the paper plates into*
> *wicker containers*)

FELICIA

What did you say to your mother—love you six? Does that mean anything special?

STEVE

Oh, it's just a dumb family joke. When Hughie was two, he couldn't really count. He couldn't really talk. And then one day he said, "Mommy, I love you six." That was as high as he could go. Mom thought it was adorable, and we thought it was hilarious. But it was one of those things that just stuck.

FELICIA

I think it's kind of sweet—

Ah, this place. As soon as dinner is over, let's get out of here. I'll show you where I'm going to bury Kevin.

FELICIA

But I love Kevin.

STEVE

We'll just slip away.

FELICIA

I can't do that. I promised Hughie I'd play chess with him.

STEVE

Well, surely you can get out of that.

FELICIA

But I don't want to get out of that.

STEVE

Phil, is there something the matter?

FELICIA

What makes you ask that?

STEVE

I have this seventh sense.

FELICIA

I liked meeting your family. I bet your father is a marvelous teacher.

STEVE

Well, he is, or everybody says he is. But what makes you think so?

FELICIA

Because he gives you his absolute attention. Look, Steve
—we are sleeping in separate rooms here, aren't we?

STEVE

Yes, definitely. Why do you ask?

FELICIA

Because I have a funny feeling that your mother knows.

STEVE

Would you care terribly if she did?

FELICIA

Yes, I would.

STEVE

But why? This is the—

FELICIA

Please, I *know* the century we're living in. But I find that I
don't want people to know what our relationship is—before I find out what it means.

STEVE

What what means?

FELICIA

Our relationship.

STEVE

Phil, you lose me when you say things like that.

FELICIA

I know. That's a risk I'm taking. Your policy—which is no

questions asked—may be correct if you are looking for the return of stolen property. But I don't think it works in real life for two people who are living together.

STEVE

Oh, my God! You're going to turn into a girl!

FELICIA

That was always in the cards.

STEVE

But why here? Why now?

FELICIA

Because suddenly you seem very different.

STEVE

Different? How?

FELICIA

Seeing you here in your own house with your own family, I realize—you're a kid, just a kid.

STEVE

(*Furious*)

Oh, I'm just a kid, am I? Damnit, you have reason to know better than that!

(HE *grabs her and kisses her roughly.*
Doorbell rings)

FELICIA

(*Breaks away*)

That is the solution to nothing.

STEVE

It's the solution to everything.

> (*Trying again, less roughly.*
> *Doorbell rings*)

FELICIA

You think that because you're twenty-two. Do you want *me* to answer the door?

STEVE

> (*Quitting and going to the door*)

Damn the doorbell! You know, they talk about wines that don't travel. Well, maybe there are people that don't travel.

> (STEVE *opens the front door to* ELSIE
> KETCHUM, *a pretty girl of twenty-*
> *two, conservatively dressed.* SHE *is*
> *hesitant and has a book in her*
> *hands.* STEVE *scarcely looks at her*)

ELSIE

Hello. Is Mrs. Cooper in?

STEVE

Yes, she's here someplace.

> (*Crossing toward the kitchen, calling*
> *back to* ELSIE)

Come right in, won't you? And watch out for those wires. My kid brother is the mad scientist and he's got extension cords everywhere.

> (*At kitchen door, opening it, and*
> *calling offstage*)

Hey, Mom, there's a girl—a young lady—here to see you.

KATY

(*From off*)
I'm making gravy. Could you find out what she wants?

ELSIE

(*Overhearing*)
Look, I don't have to see her. I can give it to you. Professor
Whitten asked me to drop this book off for Mrs. Cooper.

STEVE

(*Absently, mind still on* FELICIA)
Well, thank you very much. I'll see that she gets it.

ELSIE

You're welcome.

(ELSIE *goes.*

STEVE *crosses to kitchen, calling to*
KATY)

STEVE

It was a girl with a book for you!

KATY

(*Appearing in a flash*)
Oh, my God, yes! The book. Where is she?

STEVE

She's gone. She left the book and she left.

KATY

But she can't go! I have to see her—I mean, I've gotta . . .
I've gotta . . . I've gotta . . .

(Has rushed to the front door herself,
calling after ELSIE)

Miss Ketchum! Oh, Miss Ketchum! I'm sorry—I was busy.
Won't you come in for a minute?

ELSIE

(Off)

Thank you, but I'm running a little late!

KATY

Oh, do come in! You've got five minutes, surely.
*(*ELSIE *reappears)*

FELICIA

*(*STEVE *has been urgently whispering*
to FELICIA)

We are not going into that right now.

KATY

This is Elsie Ketchum. This is Felicia Andrayson, and my
son Steve.

ELSIE

(To STEVE, *grinning)*

Well, hi.

(More remotely to FELICIA)

Hello.

STEVE

(As it comes back now, with en-
thusiasm)

My God—Elsie! I knew, I knew, I *knew* I knew you! Where are the bangs?

ELSIE

Haven't you seen me since the bangs went? That's really a long time.

STEVE

Miss Cassidy's dancing class! Remember old Hopalong? Is she still alive?

ELSIE

Alive? The rest of us should be in such great shape. She still has her classes. Two of my cousins go.

STEVE

Hey, did you ever get married?

ELSIE

No. But why are you in such a rush to hear?
      (SHE *giggles*)

STEVE

Oh, don't you remember—you used to say you were going to get married as early as possible so you could get rid of the name Ketchum.

ELSIE

Do you know that I went for a while with a boy whose name was Borden? That would have made me Elsie Borden!

STEVE

The cow?

ELSIE

That's right. Elsie the cow.

STEVE

Thank God you didn't do that. It would have warped your whole life.

(THEY *laugh*)

KATY

I didn't realize you two knew each other.

(*Reverting to her own little plot*)

Elsie, why don't you stay and have dinner with us? It's nothing special, but—

ELSIE

Oh, I couldn't.

STEVE

Sure you could. We're having pot roast with a difference and however it turns out it'll be better than the mystery meat back at the dorm.

ELSIE

That's for sure.

KATY

Do stay.

ELSIE

All right. I'm weak, I'll stay.

(JEFF *returns from the terrace,*

118

carrying books and a sheaf of papers.
HE turns to see ELSIE)

JEFF

Miss Ketchum—is that you? Well, that's a stupid question.
Of course it's you. It's just such a surprise.
(Some of the manuscript pages fall
to the floor and HE must retrieve
them, embarrassed)
It must be clear now that I am not used to surprises—
even pleasant surprises.

KATY

(Wanting to clear the room for the
"young lovers")
Steve and Felicia, will you go out and make sure there's
enough silver. Also, drag up all the iron chairs.

STEVE

Come on, Phil, I expect you to do all the heavy work.
(STEVE and FELICIA go to the ter-
race. KATY starts to the kitchen)

JEFF

Where are you going?

KATY

Somebody's at the back door.

JEFF

I don't hear anything.

KATY

(*Firmly*)

Somebody's at the back door.

(SHE *goes into the kitchen as* JEFF
glares at her. HE *must cope with this
situation, as well as the drinks* HE
has had)

JEFF

Well, Miss Ketchum! Pink looks very pretty on you. See,
I'm saying that backwards. I'm giving the credit to pink.
I should say *you* look very pretty in pink.

ELSIE

Well, thank you, Professor Cooper.

(*Simply, not at all flirtatiously*)

But why do you keep calling me "Miss Ketchum?" In class
you always call me "Elsie."

JEFF

I guess that's true. I can only say that by some reverse,
crazy logic, in the classroom I am aware that you're a girl.
Out of the classroom I am reminded that you are a student. Now, you never heard anything more stupid than
that!

(ELSIE *giggles*)

Okay. Elsie. What brings you here?

ELSIE

Professor Whitten asked me to bring this book over to
Mrs. Cooper. He said it was important that she get it tonight.

JEFF

He asked you to *bring* it over? On a clear day he could throw it over.

ELSIE

I wondered about that.
> (KATY *returns from kitchen, with
> casserole, starts for terrace*)

KATY

Elsie is staying for dinner. It turns out she's an old friend of Stevie's.

ELSIE

Not really. We were in dancing class together. I must say I envy you, Mrs. Cooper.

KATY

Oh, really? Why?

ELSIE

Being able to read Latin.

KATY
> (*Coming back*)

What makes you think I can read Latin?

ELSIE

The book.
> (*Picking it up where* STEVE *has
> dropped it*)

KATY
> (*Finally looking at the book*)

Ovid's *Metamorphoses*.
> (SHE *opens it and it* is *in Latin*)

Of course, I don't read fluently. I have to keep a Latin dictionary right beside me.

JEFF

At all times.

ELSIE

> (*Not catching* JEFF's *tone*)

Even so—the *Metamorphoses!* I had four years of Latin in high school and I can't even read sundials!

KATY

> (*To* JEFF, *ready to bustle away*)

Listen, didn't I get the impression that you wanted to talk to Elsie about her term paper? Wouldn't this be a good time, while the rest of us are getting dinner together? You could take her into the office—

JEFF

I can't imagine where you got that idea. The paper is finished and Elsie has made all the corrections. Now, Elsie —why don't you add to the noise and confusion outside—

ELSIE

Certainly.

JEFF

Thank you. Something important has just come up.
> (ELSIE *joins the* OTHERS *on the ter-*
> *race as* JEFF *turns on* KATY *in a fury*)

You may need help. I mean psychiatric help!
> (JEFF *goes to the window off the*
> *terrace and shouts across*)

Fred! Hey, Fred!

What do you want Fred for?

JEFF

I figured you might need a Latin dictionary.
> (*Shouting out the window again*)

Fred! Hear me?

FRED

> (*From across*)

Stop yelling! What is it?

JEFF

Come to dinner! And don't tell me what you've got fixed!
The hell with it! Come to dinner! *Now!*

KATY

Talk about being the soul of hospitality—

JEFF

> (*Coming back to her, sharply*)

Look, I don't know what kind of James Bond plot you and
old Fred have hatched up. I would guess that it has something to do with bringing May and December together.
Well, you can forget it. You can put it right out of your
mind. I will have no part of it—is that clear?

KATY

Why are you dragging Fred over here?
          (FRED *has appeared from the kitchen*
          unnoticed)

FRED

Yes, why are you dragging Fred over here?

JEFF

Because I know you love pot roast.

FRED

I hate pot roast.

JEFF

Then toy with it. Roll it in your napkin. You can bring
it back to that fat dog of yours!

FRED

How did my dog get into this—and what *do* you want?

JEFF

Since you can take a large part of the credit for this gala,
I want you to be right here when it hits the fan. And I want
another drink.

KATY

You're going to get drunk.

JEFF

That certainly is my plan.
          (JEFF *has gone to the kitchen*)

KATY

(*To* FRED)

Why in heaven's name would you have her bring me a book in Latin?

FRED

I wanted you to have a sense of upmanship.

KATY

Well, what I have is a sense of being a perfect idiot!

FRED

Idiots, like the rest of us, are never perfect.

KATY

Listen, be urbane with everybody else, and forget about me.

(KEVIN *rushes in from the terrace*)

KEVIN

Hey, Mom, I think it's starting to rain.

KATY

Oh, no!

(*Low distant rumble*)

STEVE

(*Looking in from the terrace*)

Is that thunder?

KATY

Of course it's thunder.

FRED

How are you so sure?

KATY

Because we planned to eat outside. Those Indian tribes
that had rain dances, when all they had to do was set up
a picnic table—!

STEVE

Well, let's get the stuff inside.
             (*Phone rings*)

HUGHIE

             (*Bolting in from terrace*)
Hey, Mom, it's raining!

FRED

She knows.
                       (HUGHIE *answers phone. From now*
                       on, there is a constant scurry,
                       with KEVIN, STEVE, HUGHIE,
                       FELICIA *and* KATY *helping to rush*
                       things from the table on the terrace
                       into the living room. FRED *just sits*)

KATY

Kevin, take out the geraniums!

KEVIN

What?

KATY

The rain has got to be good for something. Put them out
there! Oh, thank you, Felicia.

(SHE *continues to help. Calling into*
the kitchen)
Jeff, will you please lend the hand that hasn't got a drink
in it?

HUGHIE

(*Crossing* KATY *as* SHE *heads for*
terrace)
Mom, Lorrie wants to know if I can sleep over? Can I
sleep over?

KATY

Certainly not.

STEVE

Mother. Lorrie is Lawrence Walker. He is a boy.

KATY

Oh, yes, of course. Yeah, okay, Hughie.

HUGHIE

(*Going back to phone*)
Yeah, okay, Lorrie.
(JEFF *has come from the kitchen*
and started to help, drink in one
hand, carrying the minimum in the
other)

KEVIN

(*With waterlogged paper plates*)
Mom, these plates have had it. Shall I bring them in?

KATY

No, put them in the trash can in the kitchen!

JEFF

(Bringing something from terrace;
the room is beginning to be badly
cluttered)

This is the last time I'm going to check that damn mailbox.
(JEFF *does, but there's nothing in it*)

KATY

Hey, Kevin, take one of those big plastic bags and put
it over that tub of petunias!

KEVIN

Over it? You don't mean over it?

KATY

I do mean over it. Why do I have to explain everything?
There is no little drainage hole in that tub. And if they
get too much water, the roots rot.
(KEVIN *goes to do it*)

FRED

That's why my roots are in such great shape. I *never* take
too much water.

KATY

(To FRED)
Oh, why did I listen to you? Why do I ever listen to you?

FRED

I never suggested that you invite her to dinner. That was
a little improvisation of your own.

JEFF

(*Coming back from terrace*)

Have you got everything?

STEVE

Yeah, everything but the jelly bean tablecloth!

FELICIA

(*To* FRED)

Hello!

FRED

Hello.

FELICIA

Should I put the corn in?

KATY

By all means.

FRED

(*Looking after* FELICIA *as* SHE *goes*)

She is a nice, useful girl.

KATY

But you don't know the half of it. Check with Steve.

STEVE

(*As* HE *brings in the tablecloth*)

Actually, we should have brought in this tablecloth first.

KEVIN

But that wasn't feasible.

(*Staring at the mess piled on the
table, as well as elsewhere*)

STEVE

We wanted a picnic, let's have a picnic.
(*Starting to spread cloth on the
floor*)

KATY

On the floor? I can't eat on the floor!

HUGHIE

Oh, boy, I'd love to eat on the floor. I used to wish I was
a dog so I could eat on the floor!
(*Magically, with* EVERYBODY *helping,
things are coming into place for
dinner on the floor*)

KATY

I have never pretended that my family was grand, really
grand. My father was a contractor. But we never ate on
the floor.

FRED

Tell yourself that this is a breakthrough and enjoy it.

STEVE

(*Producing a bottle of wine*)
Should we have a little wine before we serve the dinner?

JEFF

Absolutely!

KATY

Hughie, close those doors.

STEVE

Mom, would you like a pillow to sit on?

KATY

No, I would not. I mean, I would. But I wish to show that I am true blue.
(*Pointedly*)
Elsie, you sit next to Professor Cooper!

JEFF

Oh, by all means, Elsie. Do sit next to Professor Cooper. Fortunate girl—you were born under a lucky star! I'm sure you think this is all coincidence. Not at all! Somebody said—"I find it easier to believe in miracles than in a series of coincidences." What do *you* think? No matter, I shall tell you. This is the result of a conspiracy. You might even call it a caper. And if inside sources are correct, we might even trace it to—
> (JEFF *is interrupted by a blare of lightning and a loud clap of thunder. The* ADULTS *are a little frightened, but try to conceal it.* HUGHIE *is thrilled*)

HUGHIE

Wow! It feels like God just took my picture!

JEFF

(*To* KATY)
He's only eleven years old.
(*Back to* ELSIE *again*)
Elsie, as I was trying to make clear—

KATY

I'll tell you who's eleven years old—*less* than eleven years old!

STEVE

Dad, you're embarrassing Elsie.

KEVIN

And you are embarrassing Mom!

FELICIA

(*Sensing the tension and jumping in to help break it*)

Hey, listen—that lightning was pretty close. Shouldn't we be grateful?

STEVE

Or offer a *toast!*

JEFF

Absolutely, I've been waiting for this golden moment. I have been pondering something we all know. Behind every great man is a woman. But did you know behind every stupid man there is also a woman—and to that woman—

KATY

Fred, will *you please* offer the toast.

FRED

Happy Easter.

CURTAIN

Act Three

That evening. HUGHIE *and* FELICIA
*are playing chess in the window-seat
alcove. There is a sound of a basketball
bouncing, off.* JEFF *is hunting
through the drawers of an old desk,
looking for something.* KATY *enters,
all dressed up.*

JEFF
(*Looking up, finally, and noticing
her*)
Well, you're all dressed up! To what do we owe this?

KATY
I got rain all over me, and then I got pot roast all over me.
Where's Fred?

JEFF

He went home. He said after this evening he needed a week in the country or two Miltowns.

KATY

(*On her way to the front door to*
check the mailbox)
Elsie hasn't gone, has she?

JEFF

She's calling her roommate. There's nothing in the mailbox. I checked a minute ago.

KATY

Oh, Jeff, you mean you're not getting the promotion? That's rotten. You work harder than anybody!

JEFF

That's *our* opinion.
(*Going to the window*)
Kevin, I know the rain has stopped, but it's wet out there and you're going to ruin that ball!
(*We hear* KEVIN *say, "Yeah, yeah,"*
from off)

KATY

You don't care whether that ball gets ruined. You just don't want to hear it any more.

JEFF

That is absolutely correct.
(HE *is still at the window, motion-*
less)

What are you standing there for?

JEFF

There is always one last bounce.
> (*We hear the basketball bounce
> once more, off*)

Okay.

> (HE *goes back to the drawers*)

KATY

And what are you looking for?

JEFF

A wrench. Steve found a flat in my back tire and he's out there trying to change it.

KATY

You don't keep wrenches in the living room.

JEFF

I certainly don't, but my wife and children frequently do. Yep! Here we are.

> (HE *has found it, starts out the door*)

Just so you will appreciate how consistent we are in this household, I will tell you that I just found the orange juice squeezer in the trunk of the car.

> (JEFF *goes*)

KATY

> (*To herself*)

Wouldn't you think I'd have looked for that squeezer

when you consider how I hate frozen orange juice? Of course, I hate squeezing oranges worse than I hate frozen orange juice.

ELSIE

(*Coming from the phone closet and picking up her coat*)

Mrs. Cooper, there you are! I didn't want to leave without thanking you. You were so nice to ask me. I had a nifty time.

KATY

In spite of all the chaos.

ELSIE

That was kind of fun, too. All your boys are so nice, and of course, your husband is—

KATY

I know.

ELSIE

(*To* FELICIA *and* HUGHIE, *in alcove*)

Bye now. I hope to see you again.

(THEY BOTH *say,* "*So long, good-bye,*" *and* FELICIA *starts to get up*)

Please don't get up. You'll ruin your concentration.

(THEY *sit down again to their chess, and* ELSIE *turns to* KATY)

Do say good-bye to everybody else for me.

KATY

Look. Stevie and his father are fixing a flat tire. It'll only be a few minutes. Then Professor Cooper can drive you home.

ELSIE

Really, I can take the bus.

KATY

At this hour you could wait forty minutes for that bus. Anyway, I'd like to talk to you. Tell me something about yourself. Professor Cooper talks about you a lot. He says you are one of his best students.

ELSIE

Professor Cooper is a sweet, generous man, but I can't believe he ever said that.

KATY

Why not?

ELSIE

Because I'm a rotten student. The worst student in the class. I'm probably going to flunk.

KATY

(*Too quickly*)
Oh, no, you're not.

ELSIE

Actually, I won't feel too bad—if I flunk out. I'm really just taking up space. You see, I'm not brilliant like the rest of the family.

KATY

They're all brilliant?

ELSIE

There are three of us and the average I.Q. is 160. Of course that's without adding in mine, which would bring it way down. My brother had a law degree and a Ph.D. by the time he was twenty-two. My sister is a professor of Greek at Vassar.

KATY

You make it sound, somehow, like a blight.
(STEVE *enters, strolls to chess game*)

ELSIE

It sort of is. Both of them married people smarter than they were. And none of them have children. I don't think they take the pill or anything. I just think they're overbred.

KATY

Tire fixed?

STEVE

Yeah. Dad's just putting on the hub cap.

KATY

(*To* ELSIE)
You're a strange girl.

STEVE

(*To* FELICIA)
Aren't you going to use that other rook?

FELICIA

You're hovering. Don't hover.
(STEVE *wanders to the sofa, quietly
listening to his mother and* ELSIE)

140

KATY

If you don't want to be in school, what do you want to

ELSIE

I found a job I really liked last summer, but my father said it was no life for a young girl.

KATY

What was the job?

ELSIE

It was an institution for retarded children called Hillcrest. It's right outside Worcester. Technically, I was supposed to be a psychiatric aide, they've got to call them something, but all I did was play with the children.

KATY

Wasn't that kind of depressing?

ELSIE

Everybody says that. But it wasn't, not at all. You can't think how sweet they are. And how grateful they are for somebody who just sits there—and attends. By attend I mean really pay attention. The regular staff is just plain too busy for that. And when parents come to visit, mostly it's just mothers. And mostly the mothers cry, and that upsets the children. I tried to explain the job to my father, but he said, "As I see it, all you do is smile and hand out graham crackers."

KATY

But that would be a lot to do, I think.

141

ELSIE

Lots of days you wouldn't see any progress at all, and then there it would be—a tiny breakthrough. There was a little boy named Ted. He was six, maybe seven. And I knew he could talk. Not a lot, you know. But he could say words. But he didn't talk to me. I kept talking to *him* and I pretended never to notice that he didn't answer. And this went on for weeks. Then, one day, I was sitting on top of the radiator cover—I had a little two-year-old in my lap—and Ted came over. He tapped me on the knee and he said, "Lady, this is for you." And he had something squeezed up in his fist. Do you know what it was? It was a bottle top. But for me, it was a victory, a real victory. I'm sorry, you look depressed. Am I depressing you?

end scen

KATY

Not at all. But I find myself thinking that there are more important things than nonrestrictive clauses.

(JEFF *enters*)

Jeff, Elsie is ready to go. Why don't you give her a lift?

JEFF

I'd like to, but there are some reports I must get at. I'm sure Steve here would—

STEVE

(*Quick on the uptake*)

Be delighted.

ELSIE

I can take the bus, really.

142

TRAPS?

When you have a chauffeur at your service?

(*Calling to* FELICIA)

Phil, do you want to come while I drive Elsie to the dorm?

FELICIA

No, this is a very tricky moment. I am moving in for the kill.

STEVE

Okay.

(*To* ELSIE)

It's better this way. I've been wanting to have a private talk with you.

ELSIE

Oh?

STEVE

I wanted to get the lowdown. How's the *haute cuisine* at the cafeteria these days? Do they still make the chicken sandwich out of Scott paper towels and a little cold cream?

ELSIE

Yeah. But now it costs eighty-five cents.

STEVE

And the famous fried potatoes?

ELSIE

Still swimming in bacon fat.

STEVE

Swimming? They used to sink.

ELSIE

I don't know why they make them. Nobody ever eats them.

STEVE

They don't make them. They use the same ones.

ELSIE
(*To the* OTHERS, *as* SHE *goes*)
Good-bye! And thank you again!

STEVE

Dad, if the garage is open, I'll drop off that tire.

JEFF

Thank you. That's a good idea.
(STEVE *and* ELSIE *are gone*)

FELICIA

Queen to rook four.

HUGHIE

Oh, boy.

FELICIA

That's right. Check and mate.
(FELICIA *rises and goes upstairs*)

HUGHIE

Wow, I've got to figure this out.

KATY

Tell me about these reports you've got.

JEFF

They're nonexistent.

KATY

That's what I figured.

JEFF

(*Dropping his voice because of*
HUGHIE *in the alcove.* HE *doesn't drop*
it enough, though)

But you don't give up! I've been clear to the point of rude-
ness, but you don't give up!

KATY

Okay, I give up.
(SHE *goes for her coat*)

JEFF

Where are you going?

KATY

For a walk.

JEFF

For a walk—where?

KATY

Well, I shall walk to the corner, where I will have to make
the difficult decision as to whether to go to the right or to
the left. Then I will continue for another block, where I
will be faced with a whole new set of decisions. You know
something? Elsie really is a lovely child, and we were both
playing games with her. I think that's disgraceful.

JEFF

We were? You were. You were the little games-master full
of small plans and little intrigues. I was doing nothing.

145

KATY

Oh, you. You couldn't do anything if you wanted to. You're full of sound and fury signifying nothing. You have about as much initiative as an oyster!

(SHE *slams out*)

HUGHIE

(*Coming down*)
Hey, Dad, is something the matter?

JEFF

Yeah. I just got a bad report card. Well, how did the chess go?

HUGHIE

Dad, you should really play with Phil. She's too good for me.

JEFF

The last time I played with you, *you* were too good for me. Where would I get with Phil?

(FELICIA *is returning from upstairs, carrying her suitcase, which she puts down in alcove*)

FELICIA

I'm not that good. I think Hughie was being a perfect gentleman and *let* me win.

HUGHIE

(*Taking it at face value*)
Oh, no, I wasn't! Honest!

FELICIA

Professor Cooper, would you please tell Steve something important came up and I had to leave?

JEFF

You're leaving?

HUGHIE

Oh, no, please, no! You can't go! You promised you'd tape a speech for me.

FELICIA

But I can still tape the speech.

HUGHIE

I've got a tape in my bedroom. I'll get it!
(Dashing for the stairs)
What was the last play you were in?

FELICIA

The Tempest.

HUGHIE

Can you do a speech from The Tempest?

FELICIA

If that's what you want, sure.
(HUGHIE dashes upstairs)

JEFF

You don't think you should wait and tell Steve yourself?

FELICIA

No, Professor Cooper, I don't. Tell him I'll write him a letter and explain everything.

JEFF

I wish you wouldn't call me "Professor Cooper." If you could bring yourself to call me "Jeff" or even "Uh," I'd be happier and wouldn't feel so elderly.

FELICIA

But you're not elderly. I have my nerve to ask. But how old are you. Forty-five, forty-two—?

JEFF

Forty-three.

FELICIA

You're younger than Paul Newman. But I know why you *feel* older.

JEFF

Maybe you shouldn't tell me. Maybe I'm better off not knowing.

FELICIA

Because you're dealing with students. And every year they get younger—or they seem younger. Now, if you were a Supreme Court Judge you'd be a mere lad. Something else that would make you feel younger—if you were made dean. You'd be one of the youngest deans in the country.

JEFF

But I'm not going to be made dean.

FELICIA

Are you sure?

JEFF

I'm very sure.

FELICIA

Do you know the book *The Neurotic's Notebook*? There's a line in it I say to myself when I get discouraged. It goes: "Hope is the feeling you have that the feeling you have isn't permanent."

JEFF

What a bright, charming girl you are.

FELICIA

(*Looking at him*)
And you're very special, too. You have that lovely worn look that Peter Finch has.

JEFF

Are you trying to tell me that there is something good about having a worn look?

FELICIA

Yes, it's your face. There is something gentle and touching and concerned about it. It's not a usual face.
(SHE *puts her hand lightly on his cheek*)

JEFF

(*Places his hand on hers*)
My dear, pretty child. I don't know whether you are depressing me or cheering me up, but I can't risk finding out.
(*Breaking abruptly from her and going to the stairwell*)
Hey, Hughie! We're waiting! When does this program go on the air?

HUGHIE
(*Calling from above*)
I'm coming!
(HUGHIE *hurries down with a tape*
for the recorder)
I'm sorry to keep you waiting. I couldn't find my tape because Kevin piled all his stupid magazines on it. That's how he cleans out his room.

JEFF
Okay, okay—Felicia is in a hurry. Let's get started.

HUGHIE
(*To* FELICIA, *professionally*)
Do you think we should take a voice level?

FELICIA
Yes, I think so.

HUGHIE
Okay. Just say anything. Count to five.

FELICIA
(*Playing along, perfectly seriously*)
One, two, three, four, five—

HUGHIE
We'll play it back.
(*It plays back all right*)
Okay, when I raise my finger, we're starting.
(*A little embarrassed, but pleased,*
with his finger up)

This is Hugh Cooper, presenting the famous actress, Miss Felicia Andrayson, who will recite a speech from a recent play—*The Tempest*. The next voice you hear will be Felicia Andrayson.

> (*Directs his finger at her and points to the mike*)

FELICIA

> (*From memory*)

"You do look, my son, in a mov'd sort,
As if you were dismayed. Be cheerful, sir.
Our revels now are ended. These our actors,
As I foretold you, were all spirits and
Are melted into air, into thin air;
And, like the baseless fabric of this vision
The cloud-capp'd towers, the gorgeous palaces,
The solemn temples, the great globe itself,
Yea, all which it inherit, shall dissolve,
And, like this insubstantial pageant faded,
Leave not a rack behind. We are such stuff
As dreams are made on; and our little life
Is rounded with a sleep."

> (JEFF *is simply listening, with some admiration*)

HUGHIE

> (*Into mike*)

Thank you very much, Miss Andrayson.

FELICIA

(*Into mike*)

It was a pleasure, Mr. Cooper.

HUGHIE

(*Whipping tape off recorder and
jumping up*)

I'm going to take this over to Lorrie's house and play it
for him! Is he going to be impressed! Good-bye.

FELICIA

(*Offering him a handshake*)

Good-bye, Hughie. It was such a pleasure to meet you and
see your fish tank and your mynah bird—and everything.

HUGHIE

(*At door*)

When you're famous and I come backstage to see you, will
you remember me even if I'm bigger and look different?

FELICIA

You know I will.

HUGHIE

Bye. Bye, Dad!

(HUGHIE *is gone*)

FELICIA

(*To* JEFF)

Since I'm in love with the whole family, it's sort of too
bad I'm not in love with Steve.

(*Looking around*)

Now where did I stick that suitcase? Oh, yes, here we are!
>   (*Takes her suitcase from the alcove,*
>   *turning to* JEFF)
Well, good-bye—Uh—
>   (*Making her little joke*)

JEFF

Jeff.

FELICIA

Good-bye, Jeff.

JEFF

Good-bye, my dear.

FELICIA

Would it bother you to look right at me instead of at the top of my head?

JEFF

It might.
>   (HE *does look right at her*)

FELICIA

Okay, now kiss me.

JEFF

I think that could be a mistake.

FELICIA

Find out.
>   (*After a beat,* HE *kisses her, firmly*
>   *and adequately*)

See? It wasn't a mistake. It was just like I thought it would be. Again, please.

JEFF
(*Starts to kiss her and breaks away*)
Felicia, I cannot be put in the position of robbing the cradle!

FELICIA
You're not robbing the cradle. You're robbing the poor box.

JEFF
Whatever do you mean?

FELICIA
Everybody thinks I'm so pretty, so smashing. And then they get tired of me.

JEFF
I don't believe that.

FELICIA
Well, it's true. Steve brought me here this weekend just to prove that he wasn't tired of me. But he is.

JEFF
I don't believe that, either.

FELICIA
Yes, you do.

JEFF
Then he is absolutely crazy. I wouldn't get tired of you.

FELICIA

No, you wouldn't.

JEFF

Wait a minute, wait a minute, I'm getting lost here! Why are you sure I wouldn't get tired of you?

FELICIA

Because you like the fact that I am unpredictable. Young men hate unpredictable girls.

JEFF

That's their loss.

FELICIA

Are you going to kiss me again?

JEFF

Yeah.

(HE *does*)

Yeah.

(*Again*)

Yeah!

FELICIA

Jeff, what would your wife do if you came away with me for the weekend? Would she hit the roof, would she divorce you?

JEFF

Are you asking me to come with you for the weekend?

FELICIA

Yes, I am, but first I want to know how much trouble it would make.

JEFF

If you mean with my wife, I have every reason to think she would be delighted.

FELICIA

Oh? Then why not? Please come!

JEFF

Come where?

FELICIA

I'm going to drive to Nantucket. My father has a house there.

JEFF

I'm sure he'd be delighted to meet me.

FELICIA

Oh, he's not there. Nobody's there but Elena, who is seventy-two and makes the world's greatest lasagne.

JEFF

And what would Elena have to say if you turned up with a middle-aged stranger?

FELICIA

Do you understand Italian?

JEFF

No.

FELICIA

Then you'll never know what she has to say.

JEFF

Do you bring lots of—people to Nantucket?

FELICIA

I can see why you ask, but, no, I never, ever, brought anybody there. It's my favorite place in the world and I go
there when I want to be alone.

JEFF

But then why—?

FELICIA

I just had this overwhelming intuition that you would be
somebody who would be nice to be alone *with*.

JEFF

I will treasure that. My dear, I am charmed with you and
charmed with the invitation, but, of course, I can't accept.

FELICIA

You're concerned about what the boys would think.

JEFF

Undoubtedly I would go *up* in their estimation. But still—

FELICIA

Would they have to know? Don't you ever go anywhere
for a weekend alone?

JEFF

Once in a while I visit my mother.

FELICIA

Where does she live?

JEFF

In Falmouth.

FELICIA

But that's perfect! To get to Nantucket, you drive through Falmouth. I can drop you off.

JEFF

You can *what?*

FELICIA

Oh, you *are* dense! We can say that I dropped you off at your mother's.

JEFF

You are quite a little schemer.

FELICIA

That's right, I am. And you wouldn't even have to pack. My father keeps whole wardrobes of clothes in all of his houses.

JEFF

How many houses does he have?

FELICIA

Six, seven—who counts?

JEFF

It's hardly a compliment to me, but an analyst would tell you that what you are really looking for—is a father figure.

FELICIA

Two analysts have told me that. But here's the crazy thing. You're the first older man—I mean the first man older than I am—I've ever been attracted to. Don't look worried. I'm not going to coax any more. It was a wild idea, anyway.

JEFF

Actually, it was a great idea, but—

FELICIA

Yes, I know.

JEFF

You're going right now, are you?

FELICIA

Yes, it's one thing to contribute to the delinquency of a minor—but what is the opposite of that?

JEFF

I think you could contribute to anything.

FELICIA

You are so sweet. And you have the most beautiful eyes. Sometimes they're gray and sometimes they're green. But I suppose everybody tells you that.

JEFF

If you want to know the God's truth, no, nobody ever tells me that.

FELICIA
(*Extending her hand*)
Good-bye, Professor Cooper—Jeff. I'll send you a funny

card on Valentine's Day. But since I don't plan to see Steve any more, I guess I won't see you, either.

JEFF

I guess not.

FELICIA

But I want you to know something. I like you. I really and truly like you. You know, it's really easier to fall in love with somebody than to *like* them?

JEFF

Is it?

FELICIA

Oh, goodness, don't you know anything? Of course it is. Good-bye, my dear, dear Jeff.
> (SHE *kisses him lightly on the cheek*)

JEFF

If this is the last kiss I am ever going to get, it's got to be better than that.

FELICIA

Okay, I was just being careful.
> (SHE *kisses him fully,* HE *responds,*
> *and it goes on*)

JEFF

> (A *little out of breath, but definite*)
I think this would be a very good weekend to visit my mother.

FELICIA

Are you serious?

JEFF

No, I am obviously demented—but I am going. If you still—

FELICIA

Oh, yes, I still. Okay, come right this minute, just as you are. If you look back, you turn into a pillar of something.

JEFF

A pillar of the community, maybe. I won't look back, but I do have to leave a note.
> (*Scrambling through paper on the desk*)
What kind of crazy notepaper is this? It must be Hughie's. All over the top here, it says, "Good grief, it's Snoopy!"

FELICIA

I think Amy Vanderbilt would say that it was not in perfect taste for this occasion.

JEFF
> (*Having scribbled the note, takes*
> FELICIA *by the hand*)
Okay, let's get out of here before I wake up!
> (*Near the doorway, picking up*
> FELICIA's *suitcase,* HE *inadvertently*
> *trips the switch* HUGHIE *has used*
> *earlier and the amplifier immedi-*
> *ately blares out with* "*Gee, but I'd*
> *like to see that Old Gang of Mine*"

again. THEY *both jump,* JEFF *fumbles*
for the switch, can't find it, gives up)
This place is mined. Come on! I'll beat you to the car.
(THEY *bolt out, with the amplifier*
still blaring.

The lights are lowered to denote a
short lapse of time.

While the lights are lowered, the
amplified song dissolves into the ring-
ing of the telephone.

Phone is ringing steadily as lights go
up. KATY *returns from her walk, lets*
herself in hurriedly, a bit out of
breath, having heard the phone from
outside)

KATY
(*Dashing for the phone*)
I'm coming! I'm coming! Can't somebody answer this
phone?
(*Holding the closet door open with*
her back, SHE *grabs up the phone*)
Hello? Hello?
(*No answer, the party is gone. With*
a sigh KATY *hangs up and comes into*
the room, getting out of her coat)
Whoever that was, we'll never know.
(*Calling*)
Jeff? Hey, Jeff?
(*Goes to the door of his office*)

162

Jeff, you there?

> (*Puzzled by the total silence,* SHE
> *now heads for the stairwell as though*
> SHE *were going to call up, passes the*
> *desk where* JEFF *has left his note.*
> SHE *sees it and freezes. Pause*)

I will not read it. If I don't read it, it will not exist. If a tree crashes in the forest and nobody hears it, does it make a noise?

> (*Facing it*)

I guess I think it makes a noise.

> (*Picks up the note*)

Snoopy notepaper . . . when you don't care enough to send the very best . . .

> (*Reading it*)

Felicia? He's gone with *Felicia*?

> (*Pause; the irony strikes even her*)

If you think about it, it's kind of a nice twist. But I'm not going to think about it.

> (SHE *goes to the kitchen, leaving the*
> *door ajar, continuing to mutter to*
> *herself so that we can hear her*)

I'm not going to think about it, I'm not going to think about it, I am absolutely not going to think about it . . .

> (FRED *enters from the terrace*)

FRED

Both cars are gone and all through the house not a creature is stirring.

KATY

I'm stirring.

FRED

What caused the great exodus? Where is everybody?

KATY

Do you know what Steve once said when he was a little boy? When the snow melts, where does the white go?

FRED

I will take time and speculate on that. In the meantime, where *is* everybody?

KATY

Did you notice that pretty girl, Felicia—that was here with Steve?

FRED

You're damn right I did.

KATY

Well, as it turns out, so did Jeff. He's gone off with her.

FRED

Gone off with her? I don't believe it.

KATY

You don't? Well, read this . . .
          (*Hands him the note*)
It seems to be his handwriting, all right.

FRED

(*Reading*)

"Since your slightest wish is my command, I am going to spend the weekend in Nantucket with Felicia. I would prefer that you told the boys I am staying with my mother. If, however, you wish to be more honest—that's up to you. Jeff."

KATY

Do you know what is the worst thing about that note?

FRED

Everything about it is pretty rotten. What do you consider the low point?

KATY

It's signed "Jeff." He's been writing me notes for twenty-four years and he never once signed them "Jeff." He just always signed some crazy name like Tiberius Caesar or J. D. Salinger. Archibald MacLeish, that was one of his favorites . . .

FRED

Well, how do you feel?

KATY

It's strange. I don't feel anything. It's like yesterday I was using a razor blade to scrape paint off the window and I guess I cut my thumb. But I didn't feel it—you know—and then there was all this blood.

FRED

Katy, maybe it's all for the best.

Please don't sound like my father's aunt Grace. She was honest-to-God on the *Titanic*. And afterwards she said, "Maybe it all happened for the best." Some things are not for the best, Fred. And, dammit, you know it!

FRED

I keep forgetting that when you have nothing to say, you should say nothing.

KATY

The funny thing is—I sort of understand it.

FRED

How?

KATY

Jeff was asking me—was it today, was it yesterday?—all time has gone for me—but he wanted to know if I ever had dreams or fantasies about—well, about having a fling. And I said no. And I was lying.

FRED

Were you?

KATY

I didn't realize it at the time. But of course I was. Jeff takes the garbage out when he's here—but lots of times he isn't here and I take it out. And there I am in the dark with this stupid plastic bag full of garbage, and I say to myself—"He'll come." And I don't know what I mean. I don't know who *he* is.

FRED

The garbage pails are almost exactly under my window. You could always whistle.

KATY

Are you going to go back to that again?

FRED

(*Pointedly*)

When better?

KATY

It has always been your little joke that you find me ravishing.

FRED

But it wasn't a joke. I have been a little bit in love with you since we first met. And you won't remember when that was. You and Jeff were only married a couple of years and you still lived in that apartment on Lincoln Road. You invited me to dinner. I was between wives at that point. And you had on a pink linen skirt and some kind of striped shirt, and you sat on the sofa with your legs crossed under you and, for some crazy reason, you picked up a little green pillow and put it on top of your head and I thought "Wow, pow," and so forth.

KATY

I put a pillow on my head? Was I drunk? I must have looked like a nut.

FRED

You were not drunk and you looked absolutely adorable.

Even with the wear and tear, you still look adorable. To me.

Fred, be careful about being nice to me. I am tired and I am lost.

I know that. I will be careful. Can I put my arm around you? That won't commit you to anything.

> (HE *goes and puts his arm around her
> and* SHE *neither encourages him nor
> resists.*
>
> *The phone rings as he leans to kiss
> her*)

Saved by the bell. Fred, you answer it. I don't care who it is, I'm not here. Nobody's here. Just take a message.

> (*Going to closet phone*)

If nobody's here, what am I supposed to be doing?

You're the friendly neighborhood burglar.

> (FRED *disappears into the closet.*
> KATY *rests her chin on her clasped
> hands in deep concentration. Silence.
> When* FRED *comes out of the closet,*
> KATY *stands up, looks directly into*

his eyes, and then walks, almost runs,
into his arms. THEY *kiss*)

FRED

(*Softly*)
That was worth waiting for.
(*There is a pause*)
What are you thinking?

KATY

I thought I needed a drink and now I don't think I need
a drink.

FRED

It always has been better than alcohol.

KATY

(A *deep breath, then firmly but*
nervously)
Shall we go over to your place?
(HE *cocks his head quizzically*)
Well, we can't stay here.

FRED

You mean, in case one of the boys comes home. What
will they think if you're not here?

KATY

I don't know. But they won't think I'm over at your place,
that's for sure.

FRED

(*Suddenly*)
Let's have a drink.

KATY

(*Puzzled*)

Can't we have a drink over there?

FRED

What's the hurry? You afraid you're going to have second thoughts?

KATY

I already have second thoughts. I'm afraid I'll have third thoughts.

FRED

(*Going to fix one*)

I guess I want a drink right now.

KATY

What are you trying to do—nerve yourself?

FRED

Not at all. Unlike you, I do not equate this with facing a firing squad.

(A *gesture to his eyes and assuming
an attitude*)

Oh, by the way, that was Steve on the phone. Apparently there is a swinging party going on in Elsie's dorm and he wanted to come and get Felicia.

KATY

You told him?

FRED

I told him she was gone. I didn't say with whom.

KATY

Was he very upset?

FRED

His exact words were "Oh, damn, my books were in the back of her car."

KATY

That's awful!

FRED

What's awful about it?

KATY

Well, he said it was no big deal—but it should have been a bigger deal than *that*. It seems like such a lack of—well, sensibility. Do you know that poem by Edna St. Vincent Millay?
(SHE *recites*)
"Not dead of wounds, not borne
  Home to the village on a litter of branches, torn
  By splendid claws and the talk all night of the villagers
  But stung to death by gnats
  Lies love
  What swamp I sweated through for all these years
  Is at length plain to me."
(SHE *bursts into tears*)

FRED

(*Putting his arms around her gently*)
Katy, honey, don't. Please don't. You'll get a sick head-ache. Katy, look at me for a minute. Listen to me for a

minute. I'm going home by myself and you are going up to bed—by yourself.

KATY

(*Not yet over the tears*)

Well, that offer expired very quickly! Or did I simply misinterpret you all along?

FRED

Of course you didn't misinterpret me. It's just that I have had third thoughts.

KATY

What? That Jeff is your friend?

FRED

Of course, that was *the* obstacle for nineteen years. But with Jeff riding off into the sunset like this—

KATY

I wish you'd tell me what you're trying to tell me. If you have another date for the prom, that's okay.

FRED

I must remember this. It's a mistake to be ethical with women. They take it personally.

KATY

I didn't think you were ever ethical with women.

FRED

I certainly wasn't. This is my first lapse. But something has occurred to me. Today when I told you to urge Jeff to take a flier, I don't *think* I had it in the back of my mind that if he did—if he did leave—you would inevitably fall into my lap. But maybe that's what I did have in mind.

KATY

Is that very important?

FRED

Very. It's a matter of roles. I am willing to play Don Juan, but not Machiavelli. Say you understand that, sort of.

KATY

Fred, I do understand. I just feel kind of foolish as though I had worked up the courage to shoot myself and discovered the gun was empty.

FRED

Oh, the way you throw around compliments!

KATY

God, I say everything wrong.
        (KEVIN *suddenly appears on the stairwell*)

KEVIN

Hey, Mom—oh, Fred, you back?

FRED

Back but going.

KEVIN

Mom, why did you jump like that?

KATY

You startled me. There was no ghastly rock music pouring out of that room. So I figured you were out.

KEVIN

I was using my new headphones. I thought you'd be grateful.

KATY

(*With a glance at* FRED)

I am.

KEVIN

I'm starving, I'm going to get a sandwich.
(KEVIN *bolts for the kitchen*)

KATY

(*With* KEVIN *gone, turns to* FRED)
I'm grateful he doesn't know why I am so grateful he was using those headphones.
(*Giving* FRED *a little light kiss on the cheek*)
Good night, Fred, dear. When I get time to sort out my thoughts, I will appreciate—well, I'll appreciate you.

FRED

Good. And when I get time to sort out my thoughts, I'll shoot myself.
(KEVIN *pops in from kitchen*)

KEVIN

Mom, is there anything in that ice box that's top sacred? That I'm not supposed to touch?

KATY

If you mean the pot roast, there's not enough for another meal, so feel free.

FRED

Well, I've got to go. My dog is waiting up for me.
(*With quick "good nights" all
around,* FRED *goes*)

KEVIN

Where's Dad?

KATY

(*Almost jumping again*)
I—gather he decided to go to Falmouth and give Grandma
a surprise.

KEVIN

At this hour he'll give her a heart attack!

KATY

Oh, I'm sure he called.

KEVIN

But how could he go? Steve's got the car.

KATY

(*Pressed*)
I presume that Felicia dropped him off on her way to Nantucket.

KEVIN

Did Phil go? Why?

KATY

Kevin, I was absent when all these vital decisions were
made—so please spare me the third degree. I will be avail-
able for questioning at breakfast tomorrow. Okay?

KEVIN

Okay. It's just that this has been such a spooky day, and I feel it's all my fault.

KATY

How could it be your fault?

KEVIN

When I blabbed about Steve and Phil, I triggered off something. I don't know what—but something.

KATY

Don't be silly. Go make your sandwich.

KEVIN

(*About to go*)

Want half?

KATY

No, thank you, honey.

(KEVIN *comes back to her*)

KEVIN

Mom, don't let it get to you. As a mother, I'd give you 9.5 out of a possible 10.

(SHE *looks up questioningly*)

You lose five because of the way you play basketball.

(HE *grins and goes to the kitchen.*
SHE *starts to smile. Immediately we
hear* KEVIN *saying,* "Hi, Dad," *from
off.* KATY *goes rigid, then starts to
move in several directions, not
knowing where to go or what to do,*

turns and controls herself as JEFF
strides in from the kitchen. HE *tosses
a small, ordinarily wrapped package
on the table as* HE *passes*)

KATY

(*In a godawful southern accent*)
Well, lawdy, lawdy, praises be! Massuh Jeff he done come
home!

JEFF

Okay, okay.

KATY

(*Continuing*)
Us chillun was like plumb out of our skins!

JEFF

The act is lousy, knock it off.

KATY

(*Dropping the accent*)
I kind of liked it, but if you don't, okay. So, then. How
are you? How's every little thing?
(HE *doesn't answer*)
That was in my own natural voice and I still don't get an
answer.
(*More silence*)
I read your note.

JEFF

I figured you had.

KATY

Well, then.

JEFF

Well, then, what? Do I have to have written permission to come back? Presumably the house is still in both our names.

KATY

Of course, we've had very little time to do anything *legally*. I know these romances have a way of burning out, but twenty-five minutes must be some kind of a record. Did she make some ghastly mistake in grammar? Did she say, "Let's you and me" instead of "Let's you and I—"?

JEFF

How little you know, how barren your imagination! She was inflamed. I was inflamed. And then I went berserk. We were hardly out of the driveway when I hurled myself at her like a madman! I bit her neck, blood gushed. She threw me out of the car.

KATY

Oh, yes, the poor girl! I know that side of you only too well.

JEFF

Okay, what are you furious about? That I left or that I came back?

KATY

Who's furious?

JEFF

Well, there are only two of us here. By the way, how was your walk?

KATY

Just dandy. Full of interest. How was your ride?

JEFF

Actually, not too even. Her car has a stick shift and she's not quite used to it, which made the driving kind of jerky.

KATY

(*Letting the accumulated fury pour out*)

Stop this! Stop it right now! Stop it! Our whole life has come clattering down like that damn broken shade in the bedroom and you want to stand there and be as urbane as Walter Cronkite! Disaster, disaster, disaster—

(*Assuming the gracious tones of Cronkite's sign-off line*)

And *that's* the way it is, Thursday, May 30, 1972!

(*Back to rage again*)

Let's not be so goddamn civilized! Let's really talk about it or let's not talk at all.

JEFF

(*A little heated again*)

Oh, God, it was going to be high adventure and now I feel like—

(*Looking around, at wit's end, then focusing on the little package* HE *has dropped on the table*)

Open that little box.

KATY

(*Starting to*)
What is it, a coming-home present?

JEFF

No, it's the clue to my aborted romance with Miss Andrayson.

KATY

(*Removing the wrapping*)
Gelusil tablets? I don't get it.

JEFF

(*With a despairing sigh*)
Felicia had made it clear that I didn't have to pack because her father, who, you will recall, is rich beyond the
dreams of avarice, keeps entire wardrobes in all his dwell-
ings, which are numerous. So I put a pack of cigarettes in
my raincoat pocket and left. Then, as we were passing the
drugstore, I thought, "There may be thirty-two sports
jackets in that place in Nantucket, but I'll bet there won't
be any Gelusil." It occurred to me that I might need
Gelusil—not just because the pot roast was spicy, but,
what with one thing and another, I swallowed it without even chewing it. So I asked Felicia to stop and I went
into the drugstore. Marty was wrapping it up and it all came
to me—"This is insane, completely and totally insane!
Men who are swept off their feet do not stop for minor
medications!"
(*Seriously, desperately*)
Do you know how *late* it is?

(KATY, *misunderstanding, looks at
her watch*)

Oh, my God, I don't mean on your wrist watch! I mean
in our lives.

(*Quoting contemptuously*)

"Grow old with me, the best is yet to be." Do you think
Browning really believed that crap?

KATY

We're not *that* old. You make it sound like we were
senior citizens all ready for Fort Lauderdale.

JEFF

Listen, I know men my age who spend weekends with
young girls and are very humiliated because they can't
make it sexually. Well, I am awfully damn sure I could
have made it sexually. My problem is that I can't make it
psychologically. Don't you see that's worse.

KATY

No, I don't see, I don't. I really don't.

JEFF

I can't help myself. I have been programmed one way
for too long. Do you realize that for all my life—for more
than forty years!—I have been, oh good Christ, the boy
who came home on time?

KATY

Is that so terrible?

JEFF

Right now I think it is.

KATY

But who do you want to be? In your secret dreams, are you still Errol Flynn?

JEFF

(*Straight*)

In my secret dreams I had secret dreams. I don't think I will have them any more.

KATY

You shouldn't have told me that. I didn't really want to hear *that*.

> (HUGHIE *clatters in from terrace, his tape tucked under his arm*)

HUGHIE

Hi, Mom, hi, Dad!

> (THEY BOTH *grunt "Hi" without looking at him*)

Well, I have a feeling you don't want to hear a riddle.

KATY

(*Making an effort to be casual*)

I thought you were staying the night with Lorrie.

HUGHIE

Yeah, but I came back. Is Phil gone?

JEFF

Yes, she's gone.

HUGHIE

You know she recorded some Shakespeare for me? Do you want to hear it?

(*Already at the recorder*)
It's really great.

JEFF

(*In haste;* HE *doesn't want this*)
No, not tonight.

HUGHIE

(*Threading*)
It only takes a minute.

JEFF

(*Stronger*)
Some other time, Hughie.
(*But* HUGHIE *has already pressed the
button and we hear* FELICIA'S *voice
saying just one line, very audibly:*
"Be cheerful, sir, our revels now are
ended . . .")

JEFF

(*Grabbing the recorder and turning
it off*)
I *told* you not tonight! Why do you never listen? Now
go to bed. Right now! This minute! No questions. No
answers. Just go. Up. Out!
(HUGHIE *goes upstairs, muttering,
"Okay, okay."* JEFF *turns to* KATY
*whose back is to him. Her shoulders
are shaking and* SHE *is making some
kind of convulsive sound*)

183

There's nothing to cry about.
>   (HE *grabs her by the shoulders and*
>   *turns her around;* HE *is very sur-*
>   *prised*)

You're *laughing?*

KATY

>   (Nodding, *trying to suppress her*
>   *laughter*)

She's not gone, she's just away. Fortunately, we have her final message—"Be cheerful, sir, our revels now are ended." That's the thing about Shakespeare, he could always put his finger on it.
>   (JEFF *is still impassive*)

Come on, now. It *is* funny!

JEFF

They talk about having a saving sense of humor. Did it ever occur to you that we may have a losing sense of humor?

KATY

Like how?

JEFF

In the drugstore, when Marty handed me the package, I promise you that I was absolutely not thinking of you. I was really thinking what explanation I would give Felicia for stopping. So I bought a pocket comb.
>   (HE *pulls it out of his pocket*)

Exhibit B. And then inside me a little voice that was

definitely *not* my conscience said, "My God, Katy would think this was funny!" For those who come after me, I am prepared to say that a sense of humor is the *last* thing you need on a revel!

(*The phone rings.* HE *starts for it*)

KATY

Oh, don't answer it, it'll just be some kid.

JEFF

You know I can't let a phone ring. I keep thinking there's been some disaster and they need blood.

KATY

Tell them we're fresh out.

> (*While* JEFF *is in the phone closet,*
> KATY *hesitates a moment, then rushes*
> *to her purse, pulls out a compact and*
> *applies powder and lipstick, talking*
> *to herself while* SHE *does it*)

This is really and truly insane. But even on a sinking ship, people do *something*. What about that girl on the cruise ship that was going down who ran back to her cabin and turned off the bath water? Of course, that did make a certain sense. This makes no sense at all. Lipstick? What I need is plastic surgery.

> (*Hearing* JEFF *come out of the phone*
> *closet,* KATY *instinctively hides the*
> *compact behind her back, slipping it*
> *into a cigarette box behind her*)

You know what I was just thinking? Some men come home

to their wives. You may be the only man in the world who came home to his pills. The absent-minded professor to the end.

KATY

JEFF

And now the absent-minded full professor.

KATY
(*Her eyes pop*)
Oh, Jeff, was that the phone call?
(*Instantly elated,* SHE *runs to embrace him and then pulls back, embarrassed*)
That's marvelous! Was it Dean Dennis?

JEFF

Yes, the letters went out late and he thought I'd like to know today.

KATY

You look pale. How do you feel?

JEFF

Great. I feel like I just got a full pardon from the governor. I feel like the day the doctor finally cut that damn forty-pound plaster cast off my right leg! Wobbly, but free. Free! I am now a free agent.

KATY
(*Puzzled by his attitude, which is both happy and a bit fierce*)
I'm trying to follow you, but I'm not sure—

JEFF

(*Interrupting, with an odd intensity*)

Don't you see? If I didn't make it I could never leave—
never! I would just seem like a sorehead. Now that's all
changed. I could open a pizza parlor and I wouldn't seem
a sorehead. I'd just be eccentric—or maybe just plain bonk-
ers. But I could do it!

KATY

(*Catching his mood*)

Jeff. Let's do it.

JEFF

Do what?

KATY

Anything. You could even be a professor—you're a wonderful professor.

JEFF

That's my girl.

(HE *hears this last phrase*)

I didn't mean—

KATY

I know you didn't.

JEFF

(*Awkwardly putting his hand on her
shoulder*)

If I had the nerve to ask you what would you say? Are
you—my girl?

KATY

(*Shaking him off*)

Please don't rush things.

JEFF

Katy, there may not always be a bright golden haze on the meadow. But there are compensations. And once in a while you get a real hunch that there's some pattern to the pattern.

KATY

Like what?

JEFF

(*Looking straight at her*)

Like—*if* I'm the man who always comes home, I realize I am absolutely certain you're the one I want to come home to.

(KATY *bolts into his arms*)

Hey, what's this?

KATY

I'm trying to rush things.

(KEVIN *enters from the kitchen*)

KEVIN

Mom?

(KATY *and* JEFF *break apart*)

KATY

(*Brightly, as casually as possible*)

Hi, Kevin! Did you get something to eat?

KEVIN

I had a pot roast sandwich with horseradish and then I cleaned up the rest of the chili.

KATY

That should keep body and soul together until breakfast.

KEVIN

Yeah, but it was kind of much. And I can't find any Gelusil!

JEFF

Oh, you lucky boy! You have come to the right person.
(*Flying to the package* HE *has brought*)
Like those flashlight batteries, I am ever-ready! Here, my boy—relief is at hand!
(HE *throws him the Gelusil*)

KEVIN

Oh. Thank you!
(*To* JEFF, *who is starting to turn down the lights*)
Night, Dad.
(*Gives* KATY *a light kiss on the cheek and starts for stairs*)
Night, Mom. Love you six.
(KEVIN *goes upstairs*)

KATY

(*Philosophically*)
That certainly was a pot roast with a difference.

> (*Noticing that* JEFF *has turned off*
> *various lamps*)

Leave some light for Stevie.

JEFF

> (*Nodding*)

Now how do I get the Gelusil back from Kevin?

KATY

There's some in the pocket of your pajamas. I always put two in the pocket of your pajamas. You never noticed?

> (THEY *have virtually finished their*
> *cleaning up and closing down and are*
> *near the foot of the staircase*)

JEFF

Of course I noticed. It just went out of my head. What *is* the matter with me?

KATY

> (*Almost fondly*)

Everything.

JEFF

Katy, want to know something?

KATY

Yeah.

JEFF

I love you seven.

KATY

Make that eight and you've got yourself a deal.
> (HE *takes her hand and* THEY *start up the stairs*)

JEFF

> (*On the way up*)

Eight—nine—ten—
> (*The phone rings.* KATY *almost makes a move to turn down to answer it, but* JEFF *keeps her hand firmly and continues counting as* THEY *go up*)

eleven—twelve—
> (THEY *are gone. The phone just keeps ringing*)

CURTAIN

DATE DUE

FEB 21 1997		
JUN 15 1998		
JAN 0 4 2002		
JUN 15		
MAR 0 2 2006		
		Printed in USA